M000195615

The Forgotten Army

THE FORGOTTEN ARMY

The American Eighth Army in the Southern Philippines 1945

ROBERT M. YOUNG

Westphalia Press

An Imprint of the Policy Studies Organization

Washington, DC

2020

THE FORGOTTEN ARMY
All Rights Reserved © 2020 by Policy Studies Organization

Westphalia Press
An imprint of Policy Studies Organization
1527 New Hampshire Ave., NW
Washington, D.C. 20036
info@ipsonet.org

ISBN: 978-1-941755-18-1

Cover and interior design by Jeffrey Barnes
jbarnesbook.design

Daniel Gutierrez-Sandoval, Executive Director
PSO and Westphalia Press

Updated material and comments on this edition
can be found at the Westphalia Press website:
www.westphaliapress.org

I dedicate this book to Cali, a precious puppy that was taken from my family far too early. You are dearly missed and will remain with us forever.

Table of Contents

Preface

In the spring of 1945, the end of the Second World War was but a few months away. Yet, vicious fighting continued unabated. Nowhere was that more evident than in what the United States termed the Southwest Pacific Area (SWPA). The US forces in that part of the war, under the overall command of General Douglas MacArthur, continued to fight a skilled, tenacious, and fanatical enemy on the main Philippine island of Luzon. The US Sixth Army, under the command of General Walter Krueger, was fighting and toiling in the mountains of northern Luzon, for little tactical or strategic purpose. In need of rest, reinforcement, and relief, they would instead continue to see their strength and morale wither away. Reinforcements were available, but MacArthur used those men to create a new army, the Eighth, to invade and capture the islands of the Southern Philippines. MacArthur selected General Robert Eichelberger, a commander he knew well from previous SWPA operations, to lead this new force. The Eighth Army served with honor and distinction.

I

The President of the United States ordered me to break through the Japanese lines and proceed to Corregidor to Australia for the same purpose, as I understand it, of organizing an American offensive against Japan, the primary purpose of which is the relief of the Philippines. I came through and I shall return.[1]

—General Douglas MacArthur, 1942

General Douglas MacArthur is a very recognizable name in US military history. His family had fought during the American Civil War; he had graduated from West Point, served with honor and distinction during World War I (WWI), rose to Superintendent of the US Military Academy, and then became Army Chief of Staff for President Herbert Hoover. During his tenure as the Army's top officer, he advised the President to use force to disperse the "Bonus Army," a peaceful gathering of WWI veterans who had fallen on hard economic times during the Depression and were seeking early payment of their bonuses. This shameful act led, either directly or indirectly, to President Franklin Roosevelt sending MacArthur to the Philippines to serve as the military advisor to the US territory. He was restored to active duty when World War II (WWII) began.

While in the Philippines, General MacArthur, in addition to his role as a Philippine military advisor, also bore responsibility for the US Army and air power stationed in the vast island chain. Much was made in military circles at the time and in historical circles since about responsibility for the debacle of December

---

1   http://monumentaustralia.org.au/themes/conflict/ww2/display/51790-%22-i-came-out-of-bataan-and-i-shall-return-%22-.

7, 1941 at Pearl Harbor. Yet, little attention is paid to the debacle that occurred hours later in the Philippines. MacArthur was informed of the Japanese attack shortly after it happened, yet, when Japanese bombers appeared over the main US air base of Clark Field on the island of Luzon, a fate similar to that of the planes in Hawaii happened. MacArthur's planes were caught on the ground and his forces were quickly outflanked by Japanese units landing at will. In fairness, there was little MacArthur or anyone else could have done at this point to stop the Japanese, but his planes should have been dispersed. No reinforcements were available, the closest US base was thousands of miles away, and US air and naval power were nonexistent. The Philippines were lost. As all collapsed around him, MacArthur was personally saved by President Roosevelt, who ordered him to Australia to begin the process of rebuilding the US military presence in the Pacific. Before speeding away on a Patrol Torpedo boat, he made the famous boast that would become the basis of the Pacific War, "I shall return." He also received America's highest military honor for losing the Philippines. The first few months of the war were not kind to the United States' situation in the Pacific. The Japanese had taken the Philippines, the Dutch East Indies, and most of Southeast Asia, and controlled the vast maze of Pacific islands to the doorsteps of Midway, a small island several hundred miles west of Hawaii. President Franklin Roosevelt believed that America needed a hero and recommended MacArthur for the Medal of Honor. The citation read:

> For conspicuous leadership in preparing the Philippine Islands to resist conquest, for gallantry and intrepidity above and beyond the call of duty in action against invading Japanese forces, and for the heroic conduct of defensive and offensive operations on the Bataan Peninsula. He mobilized, trained, and led an army which has received world acclaim for its gallant defense against a tremendous superiority of en-

emy forces in men and arms. His utter disregard
of personal danger under heavy fire and aerial
bombardment, his calm judgment in each cri-
sis, inspired his troops, galvanized the spirit of
resistance of the Filipino people, and confirmed
the faith of the American people in their armed
forces.[2]

The sheer absurdity of that citation defies explanation. MacArthur faced enormous odds and had no hope of reinforcement
or relief. But heroic defensive and offensive operations? General Jonathan Wainwright conducted a heroic, hopeless stand on
the Bataan Peninsula and spent the next three years in a Japanese
prison camp. There were no further offensive operations of any
kind worth mentioning. Further, in the hours after Pearl Harbor,
MacArthur took no steps to disperse his aircraft at Clark Field
and they were caught on the ground, eliminating his one major
asset capable of stunting Japanese actions. General Walter Short,
the Army commander in Hawaii, was relieved of his command
for allowing his planes to be caught on the ground. Admiral Hus-
band Kimmel was relieved of his command of the Pacific Fleet.
MacArthur received the Medal of Honor. His boast of returning
to the Philippines dominated the US strategic debate in the Pacific for the next three years.

When MacArthur reached Australia after fleeing the Philippines, there was little to work with. Nevertheless, US forces were
quickly thrust into action. To the north of Australia is the world's
second largest island, New Guinea. Should the Japanese occu-
py New Guinea, especially the harbor of Port Moresby on the
island's southern coast, Australia itself would be threatened. In
May 1942, the Japanese attempted a seaborne invasion of New
Guinea, with Port Moresby the ultimate prize. US signal intelligence figured this out and two US aircraft carriers, the *Lexington*

2 http://www.homeofheroes.com/moh/citations_1940_wwii/macar
thur_douglas.htm.

and *Yorktown*, sailed to meet them. The resulting engagement, the Battle of the Coral Sea, was a tactical victory for the Japanese, but a strategic victory for the United States. America lost the *Lexington* and the *Yorktown* suffered extensive damage. US carrier planes sank the *Shoho*, a light Japanese aircraft carrier, and devastated the air groups of two Pearl Harbor veterans, the *Shokaku* and *Zuikaku*, putting them out of action for several months. The Japanese force turned for home, their commander loath to risk his precious ships despite the fact he outnumbered his enemy. During the fall of 1942, a Japanese force landed on New Guinea's northern coast and proceeded to make a treacherous overland march toward Port Moresby. Jungle, disease, the Owen Stanley mountains, and starvation—all contributed to the virtual skeletons that stopped short of Port Moresby at Buna. Buna, an old coconut plantation, now had a couple of vital airstrips that could threaten Port Moresby and even Australia. With only the 32nd and 41st Infantry Divisions (IDs) available, both National Guard units completely unprepared for jungle warfare, MacArthur made the controversial decision to commit his meager force to the capture of Buna in November 1942.

The 32nd ID undertook the preponderance of the fighting and suffering in the coming battle. The Japanese constructed sturdy pillboxes on all the approaches to the airstrips and developed positions throughout the dense jungle. Attack after attack was repulsed. MacArthur's historic impatience appeared and the main casualty was the 32nd's commander, General Edwin F. Harding. Harding immediately realized that his infantry alone could do little against the stout enemy positions. He needed and pleaded for heavy weapons, especially tanks. His entire division had but one artillery piece and it had the wrong type of ammunition for a jungle environment.[3] Harding's pleas went unanswered by MacArthur, who placed the blame on poor leadership and weak soldiers.

---

3   The lone American artillery piece was initially outfitted with proximity fuses, which exploded on contact. Given the large amounts of jungle growth the Japanese placed on their positions, the artillery did little more than blow everything around. Delayed action fuses did not arrive until later in the battle.

Despite never visiting the ground, despite their own intelligence underestimates of Japanese strength and capabilities, and despite sending his men into a battle they were unprepared and underequipped for, MacArthur relieved Harding. His replacement was General Robert Eichelberger, a commander who would earn the nickname "MacArthur's Fireman" for the multiple times he had saved his boss' campaigns. Eichelberger had actually evaluated the 32nd in the summer of 1942. He had rated them "barely satisfactory," noting their lack of physical acclimation to a jungle environment and inexperience in night problems and the "general art of soldiering."[4] He instituted a rigorous training program that had yet to bear fruit at the time the 32nd was committed to battle. When told he was on his way to Buna to save the situation, Eichelberger received MacArthur's farewell message:

> I want you to go to Buna and capture it. If you do not do so I don't want you to come out alive and that applies to your Chief of Staff also. Do you understand Bob! Time is of the essence! I want you to relieve Harding Bob. Send him back to America. If you don't do it I will. Relieve every regimental and battalion commander. Put corporals in command if necessary. Get somebody who will fight. When do you want to start Bob?[5]

It was a really inspiring send off. Eichelberger went to Buna to fix the mess MacArthur had created.

Mindful of his superior's orders, Eichelberger launched an attack against the airfields soon after arriving at Buna. It was, as those previously launched, stopped cold. Eichelberger completely understood the feelings of helplessness that must have encumbered General Harding. He steadfastly refused to launch any further attacks until his lone artillery piece received the proper ammuni-

---

4   Robert Young, *They Too Fought The Japanese* (New York: The City University of New York), 10–14.

5   *Introduction to the Eichelberger Papers* (North Carolina: Duke University).

tion and his men secured armored support. It raises the question of how an entire US ID had but one 105-mm gun in its entire inventory. The 32nd ID was clearly not ready for combat, either in the battle readiness in a jungle environment of their men or their basic equipment. Several M3 Stuart light tanks arrived soon after, completely changing the course of the battle.

The Stuarts allowed the infantry of the 32nd to finally overwhelm the bunkers that had frustrated them for nearly two months. The Stuarts were small compared to the giants that would become famous in WWII and had only a 37-mm gun. But, the Japanese had no armor available and no anti-tank weapons of any note. Buna and its airstrips fell in January 1943. It could have been November 1942 had MacArthur provided these same tanks when General Harding had initially requested them. With Buna secure, what next? MacArthur's ground forces would reenter the fray during the spring of 1944 after spending the preceding months training and bolstering their strength. While his qualities as a commander or person can be questioned, MacArthur's inherent military genius cannot. Historians have lauded the island hopping campaign across the Central Pacific by Admiral Chester Nimitz as an act of brilliance. MacArthur launched a similar campaign along the northern coast of New Guinea that placed his forces in perfect position to strike at the Philippines and fulfill his promise to return.

MacArthur's plan to hop from point to point along New Guinea's northern coast was brilliant. Major enemy garrisons were outflanked and left to wither away. All operations could count on land-based air support. Yet, problems existed on the tactical level, primarily limited ground forces and impatience. Nevertheless, this masterful drive across New Guinea never involved more than the elements of five IDs. Several of these divisions were involved in multiple operations simultaneously. The pattern that emerged was initiating new battles before previous ones had ended. This stretched MacArthur's limited manpower unnecessarily and prevented support and reinforcements when needed. A new US

Army, the Sixth, under the command of General Walter Krueger, was created to manage the various divisions involved in the New Guinea campaign. Krueger often showed the same impatience as his boss but had to manage both the Army and MacArthur's meddling and egotistical decisions at the same time. Fortunately, the first operation of this campaign, at Hollandia, faced no real obstacles and resulted in a resounding success.

Hollandia was attacked and secured in April 1944. It was lightly defended and the perfect position from which to stage future operations, possessing several excellent airfields and a large port. The seizure of Hollandia cut off an entire Japanese army in eastern New Guinea, although that army reentered the picture several months later. *ULTRA*, the top-secret name for the Allied effort to break the Japanese and German military codes, informed MacArthur that Hollandia was lightly defended and that he could also cut off an entire Japanese army by landing there. This was a brilliant campaign, but it did have some quiet help. With Hollandia secure, the Sixth Army set its sights on Wakde, a small island off of New Guinea's northern coast.

Wakde was as close to perfect as any military operation of WWII. The small island had a vital airstrip and elements of the 41st ID were tasked with its capture. The 41st had entered the Buna operation in its final days and in the year that followed they honed their skills in both jungle warfare and combined arms, small-unit actions. Unlike Buna, modern tanks and artillery were available in abundance. It took the 41st two days, May 18-19, 1944, to secure the island. US casualties were light. The entire Japanese garrison of several hundred men was eliminated. Across the water lay Sarmi and the infamous Lone Tree Hill.

Given that Wakde's position was very close to New Guinea itself, General Krueger worried that Japanese forces could still threaten it. The 158th Regimental Combat Team (RCT) landed on New Guinea and on May 23, 1944, began its advance west. Several times the advance was blunted by stout Japanese defenses and heavy jungle, but the 158th continued to edge forward. Lone Tree Hill, a point several thousand yards west of the Tirfoam River and the last enemy position before a vital airfield, stood in the way.

Lone Tree Hill, so dubbed by the US infantry who fought for it, was approximately 175 feet high, 1,200 yards long, and 1,100 yards wide.[6] It was steep, rocky, and had a twisting stream (Snaky River) flowing before its eastern face. A defile also existed between Lone Tree Hill and the nearby Mt. Saskin. Many fought and died in that defile. For several days, beginning on May 26, the 158th RCT tried to secure Lone Tree Hill. After only two days, the unit sustained nearly 300 casualties, dead and wounded, and had accomplished little. They were pulled off the line because the 158th RCT was earmarked for the invasion of Noemfoor, a point 300 miles further west. The Sixth ID would replace the 158th but not launch their first attack until nearly a month later, on June 20. This began a pattern in MacArthur's operations: a new campaign would start before an earlier one had finished. He had to keep up with the pace of Nimitz's drive across the Central Pacific. Lone Tree Hill and the surrounding area should have been secured before continuing the move west. When new operations began, they took with them naval and air support as well as potential reinforcements. The Sixth toiled in the heat and jungle of Lone Tree Hill for 10 days before it was finally secured. Reinforcements that could have brought a swift end to the battle were instead fighting on the island of Biak.

Biak is another island off New Guinea's northern coast. Substantially larger than Wakde, it contained three major airfield complexes. These airdromes were needed not only to support MacArthur's New Guinea operations, but also Nimitz's operations against the Marianna Islands, scheduled to commence on June 15. The landings on Biak by the 41st ID began on May 27. The operations in the Sarmi area and specifically Lone Tree

---

6   Young, *They Too Fought The Japanese*, 91.

Hill were still in progress. Each operation could have gone both quicker and easier if they had been the only one progressing at any given point. Biak was not officially secured until July 22.

Biak was a mountainous Pacific island, boiling hot, and abounded with natural coral. The coral and caves of Biak allowed its Japanese defenders to give the Americans the airfields while still denying them their use, as they dominated the high ground overlooking them. MacArthur actually declared Biak secure on June 21. He had the airfields but was unable to support Nimitz's operations or his own because they were not operational. Thousands of bombs, tens of thousands of artillery and mortar rounds, and finally thousands of gallons of gasoline poured into crevices within the coral and caves and then electrically ignited finally ended the murderous fighting on Biak. MacArthur was edging closer and closer to his return to the Philippines. However, another fight that he had not anticipated was brewing far to his east.

The Hollandia landings had cut off the Japanese 18th Army in eastern New Guinea. A total of 55,000 men were all but forgotten by MacArthur and even their superiors in Tokyo. That 55,000-man force, facing starvation or eventual surrender if they remained static, began moving west, hoping to link up with other Japanese units once passing the narrow Drinumor River. *ULTRA* informed MacArthur and Krueger of this movement, a movement that, if successful, would place the airfields and storage facilities in the Hollandia/Aitape area in significant peril. Yet, the US generals did as little as possible to meet this impending threat. To shift forces east would have dissipated efforts on Biak, at Sarmi, and future operations further west at Noemfoor, Sansapor, and Morotai. MacArthur even knew the general day of the attack, July 10, and still made no major effort to bolster his forces. It was not even called a defense. Instead, it was referred to as a "covering force" operation. Two regiments of the 32nd ID and the understrength 112th Cavalry Regiment, later supplemented by elements of the 31st ID (one regiment of approximately 3,000 men), were all that stood before the 55,000 men of the Japanese 18th Army.

Five infantry battalions (approximately 800 men each) were supposed to be waiting for the Japanese when they attacked. They were responsible for five miles of jungle-infested front, an impossible task. Krueger, through *ULTRA*, knew where the Japanese were (*ULTRA* information did not go below Army commanders), but could not imply that information to his subordinates. He ordered a two-battalion reconnaissance in force along the flanks of the US line several days before the anticipated Japanese attack. Unfortunately for the three infantry battalions still covering the Drinumor, *ULTRA* did not take into account the thick jungle of New Guinea. The two battalions that deployed for the reconnaissance in force never saw the Japanese. The jungle was so thick and overwhelming that two battalions could easily miss an entire army. The 18th Japanese Army attacked a very weak line when they came screaming out of the jungle on a humid July night.

The US line had substantial artillery support and the guns had previously registered key points along the line, as *ULTRA* told them where the Japanese would attack. The sheer weight of numbers found holes in a severely undermanned, extended line, despite the roar of the US guns. Eventually, the US forces fell back, a decision for which General Krueger loudly criticized his commanders. The line was stabilized and over the following weeks, the Japanese 18th Army was destroyed, its remnants scattered into the jungle. It was a US victory, but it need not have been such a difficult victory.

Reinforcements would have made this a far easier task. MacArthur and Krueger were both aware of where the Japanese attack would take place. Another infantry regiment or, even better, a full ID would have made all the difference. With operations occurring concurrently on Biak and Sarmi and with future battles staging further west on New Guinea, help would come in small increments. Perhaps MacArthur was hesitant to surrender the headlines to Nimitz as he successfully secured the Marianna Islands. Perhaps MacArthur feared the final defeat of his winning the war throughout the Philippines argument if he could not point to continuous progress. Despite the aforementioned campaigns and the inherent difficulties within them, by the close of July 1944, New Guinea was essentially secure. Several smaller operations still occurred, but the anticipated landings in the Philippines scheduled for early 1945 now seemed unnecessarily far into the future. It was agreed in Washington that the momentum MacArthur possessed should be exploited. Circumstances and a lack of Japanese opposition moved up the timetable for the landings. Admiral William "Bull" Halsey's Third Fleet began attacking Mindanao, an island in the Southern Philippines, in September and was shocked at the sparse Japanese opposition. Attacks against the Visayans, a small group of islands between New Guinea and the Philippines, were also very successful and largely unopposed. Halsey then suggested that the timetable for the Philippine invasion be moved up and his request was approved.[7] In October 1944, MacArthur affirmed his vow to return to the Philippines when General Krueger's Sixth Army landed on the island of Leyte.

The Philippine island of Leyte is most famous for history's greatest naval battle, the Battle of Leyte Gulf. When MacArthur's forces approached Leyte, the Japanese high command knew that the war was beyond hope if US forces controlled the Philippines. The fact the Japanese believed this and sortied the best of their navy to Leyte bolstered MacArthur's argument in support of this operation. This was also the time for the great naval battle the Japanese had anticipated for the entire war. This was a battle of annihilation between large capital ships. Their vital supplies (oil, metal, rubber, and food) came from conquered territories in Southeast Asia. US submarines and aircraft operating from Filipino bases could strangle the lines of supply needed by the Japa-

---

7   Dan van der Vat, *The Pacific Campaign* (New York: Simon & Schuster, 1991), 346.

nese military and civilian population. The major remaining units of the Imperial Japanese Navy sortied for Leyte. Despite several mistakes made by US naval commander Admiral Halsey, the Japanese fleet was savaged, never again to pose a threat to US forces.[8] The landings on Leyte were an overwhelming success and after vicious fighting, the island was secured. The main Philippine island of Luzon was the next obvious target.

Luzon, the largest island of the vast Philippine archipelago, was also home to its capital city, Manila, and the largest Japanese army east of China. Over 250,000 soldiers under the command of General Tomoyuki Yamashita awaited MacArthur and Krueger's Sixth Army. It was a battle the Japanese commander knew he could not win. Yamashita hoped to delay the inevitable as long as possible, digging into the rugged mountains and jungles of northern Luzon, allowing MacArthur's forces to attack him. Should MacArthur not attack his entrenched forces but instead satisfy himself with the capture of Manila and the surrounding areas, which Yamashita did not intend on defending, the Japanese commander could do little to influence events. He lacked supplies, air support, transport, and any hope of reinforcement or relief. He was in the exact same situation as MacArthur in 1942, but had considerably more strength, at least in numbers. The only way Yamashita could affect events was if MacArthur ordered his forces to attack the Japanese in Luzon's rugged northern mountains, which is precisely what happened.

Before even discussing the Eighth Army's role in the Philippine campaign, an examination of the necessity of the campaign as a whole is necessary. The Eighth Army performed magnificently once it entered the war. Sadly, it was not needed here. No US forces were needed in the Philippines to win the war against Ja-

---

8   Halsey fell for a Japanese decoy, empty aircraft carriers, and pursued with most of his battle fleet a portion of the Japanese fleet away from Leyte. Japanese tepidness, severe acts of bravery by minor US naval units, and some luck saved the landing force and allowed other forces to pound the Japanese Navy to impotence.

pan. A vicious strategic debate concerning how best to win the war in the Pacific raged almost to the moment US forces landed in the Philippines in October 1944. The debate followed two principle avenues of approach: a drive across the Central Pacific led by the Navy and a return to the Philippines. The Navy, with its massive aircraft carrier-led fleet and several Army infantry and Marine divisions, had a more direct line to Japan and required fewer ground forces. Macarthur could not and would not accept the Central Pacific as the most direct route to Japan. The Navy's highly mobile carrier and amphibious forces, cruising freely across the Pacific with their floating logistical bases, could advance further and faster and bypass enemy strongpoints far more readily than the forces of MacArthur, who was tied to land-based airfields.

MacArthur's arguments had merit, both militarily and morally. Militarily, they just were not the best option; however, this option should not have been completely disregarded. Japan was dependent on Southeast Asia for their vital natural resources. Oil, rubber, metals, etc. all traveled by ship northward along the Asian coast toward the Japanese home islands. Should that lifeline have been severed, Japan could have been broken, possibly without a direct invasion. The Philippines were the ideal location to interdict the supply line, a point MacArthur repeatedly stated.[9] The Philippines were also perfect for building bases or even enhancing old US positions, like Clark Field (a vast air base on southern Luzon), bases from which an invasion of Japan could be launched. As with Admiral Nimitz's invasion of the Marianas in June 1944, the Japanese recognized how precarious their strategic situation became with the US occupation of the Philippines.[10] They sent the Imperial Navy, which survived the Battle of the

---

9   Michael Schaller, *Douglas MacArthur: The Far Eastern General* (London: Oxford University Press, 1989), 99.

10 When American amphibious forces approached the Marianna Islands in June, the Japanese sortied their fleet and its new and veteran aircraft carriers. The Marianas were located within heavy bomber range of Japan. The result,

Philippine Sea, to contest the US landings on the island of Leyte in October 1944. The Battle of Leyte Gulf, history's largest naval battle and an overwhelming US victory, to some degree validates MacArthur's claim as to the value of the Philippines. Why else would the Japanese send all the major units of their fleet, devoid of naval air cover, against the more powerful US Navy?

The argument that occupation of the Philippines would sever Japan's economic ties with Southeast Asia is superfluous, that connection had been severed before the US Sixth Army ever landed on Leyte. US submarines had savaged Japan's merchant fleet, depriving the military and home islands of many of their most basic commodities, especially oil. A total of 603 Japanese merchant ships went to the bottom of the ocean in 1944 alone. Luzon itself was not even invaded until January 1945. These 603 ships totaling 2.7 million tons, over half of Japan's merchant fleet, also took 60 percent of Japan's bulk imports with them.[11] These submarines were based in Hawaii and remained so until the end of the war. Further, Okinawa was a far better base from which to invade Japan, only 350 miles from the Japanese home islands, as compared to the roughly 1,200 mile trek from the Philippines. The Marianas could serve the same purpose as the Philippines and were already occupied, with major air bases. A Japanese army of 110,000 defended Okinawa. While undoubtedly a significant force, it was barely one third of the Japanese army in the Philippines. MacArthur had conducted his own variation of an island-hopping campaign across New Guinea's northern coast during the spring and summer of 1944. He had bypassed strongpoints and even cut off an entire Japanese army of 55,000 men when his forces landed at Hollandia. Rabaul, the powerful Japanese base on New Britain, north of New Guinea, was MacArthur's main objective until his New Guinea campaign began. It was a powerful base with a

---

the naval battle of the Philippine Sea, was a battle that was an overwhelming US victory and saw the end of Japanese naval air power. By the end of July, the islands were secure and vast bomber bases were under construction.

11 Dan van der Vat, *The Pacific Campaign*, 375.

significant defending force. To secure Rabaul would have undoubtedly been a long and costly process. Rather than subject his troops to a potential bloodbath, MacArthur's Fifth Air Force isolated and battered Rabaul to the point of uselessness. It was a brilliant campaign and one that demonstrated the flexibility and cunning of a great commander. Why was that not displayed here? The recapture of the Philippines was personal to MacArthur and he used his considerable personal clout to guarantee a campaign that was not needed.

Morally, a strong case can be made for this campaign. MacArthur had spent many years in the Philippines prior to WWII and grown very fond of the Filipino people. Many of those suffering under Japan's iron fist were members of his command, the command he had left in 1942. While he may have been egotistical and self-centered, he felt for those in the Japanese prisoner of war and concentration camps. Later in the campaign, when word came to him that an opportunity to save US prisoners presented itself, he jumped:

> I was deeply concerned about the thousands of prisoners who had been interned at the various camps on Luzon since the early days of the war.
>
> Shortly after the Japanese had taken over the islands, they had gathered Americans, British, and other Allied nationals, including women and children in concentration centers without regard to whether they were actual combatants or simply civilians. I had been receiving reports from my various underground sources long before the actual landings on Luzon, but the latest information was most alarming. With every step that our soldiers took toward Santo Thomas University, Bilibid, Cabanatuan, and Los Banos, where these prisoners were held, the Japanese soldiers guarding them had become more sadis-

tic. I knew that many of these half-starved and ill-treated people would die unless we rescued them promptly. The thought of their destruction with deliverance so near was deeply repellent to me.[12]

The famous Los Banos Raid would follow immediately thereafter. The Filipino people, US prisoners—all were in a desperate way. That was a valid argument for action, one that could have and should have been made more forcefully.

US territory was attacked and occupied by the Japanese during WWII. Wake Island, Guam, Attu, Kiska in the Aleutians, and the Philippines were all victims of Japan's incredible success in the Pacific war's first six months. The basic duty of government, of all government, is to protect its people. Attu and Kiska possessed no military value and were only occupied by the Japanese to distract US attention away from their intended target of the island of Midway in June 1942. Yet, in the spring of 1943, both islands were invaded and secured. Attu was a very costly operation. Guam was retaken during the Marianas operation. Wake was handed back after Japan's surrender on September 4, 1945, a victim of the central Pacific island hopping strategy. The Philippines were US territory. Even if it made little sense militarily and a far stronger argument existed for the Philippines than either the Aleutians or Wake, the US government has a legal and moral obligation to its people. This should have been all that MacArthur stated. It may not have carried the day, but it would have been unassailable. Political threats and nonsensical paranoia are trumped by reality, both legal and moral. The thousands of US prisoners and millions of Filipino civilians living under the sword of Japanese brutality deserved a voice as well.

In the end, President Roosevelt did not make a decision. Both the drive across the central Pacific and MacArthur's return to the

---

12 Douglas MacArthur, *Reminiscences* (Maryland: Naval Institute Press, 1964), 198.

Philippines continued. It is testament to the immense strength and resources of the United States that both campaigns were adequately supported and ultimately successful. A return to the Philippines was not as militarily decisive as the central Pacific drive. It should have been, as historian Dan van der Vat stated, "a one-horse race with a single jockey."[13] Nevertheless, MacArthur's personal honor, as he saw it, could now be redeemed. A significant Japanese army defended the Philippines. Its entire strength need not have been confronted. Once the landings started at Leyte in October 1944, it was inevitable that Luzon, the main island of the Philippines and home to the capital city of Manila, would follow. A limited landing on Luzon would have achieved all the strategic purposes (ability to interdict Japanese lines of communication and supply, establishing staging areas for an invasion of Japan), which MacArthur had previously detailed when pushing for this operation. However, when MacArthur returned to the Philippines, he meant all of the Philippines. No matter the strategic irrelevance, no matter the enemy strength, or the weakness of his own forces, the Japanese would not be permitted to control any Filipino territory.

Once the Sixth Army landed on Leyte, the strategic debate ended. MacArthur had returned to the Philippines and the drive across the central Pacific continued. One was not sacrificed for the other. However, the conduct of the Filipino campaign itself is open to harsh scrutiny. The operations for which the Eighth Army was responsible in the Southern Philippines became unnecessary once the landings on Leyte occurred. Every Filipino island and Japanese garrison south of Leyte was outflanked and cut off from any hope of reinforcement or relief. That will be examined in a bit. After the successful operation on Leyte, MacArthur abandoned the tactical genius he had exhibited early in his military career and during the New Guinea campaign. Several divisions of the Sixth Army paid a heavy price for this failure.

---

13 Van der Vat, 321.

Luzon was the obvious objective of the Sixth Army after Leyte's capture. It was the largest island of the Philippines and Manila possessed the port and staging areas necessary to support a future invasion of Japan. The Sixth Army, at the beginning of the campaign, had nine divisions (seven infantry, one cavalry, one airborne). They began landing on Luzon's western coast in Lingayen Gulf in January 1945. Their immediate objective was Manila.

The Sixth Army reached Manila fairly quickly. Two of its divisions, the 37th Infantry and 1st Cavalry, spent the next several weeks engaged in some of modern history's most destructive urban combat. Stalingrad justifiably holds a place in historical lore for the death and mayhem that can result from prolonged fighting between determined forces equipped with modern weapons in an urban environment. Manila was no different. Over one half a million of its people died during the fight between a fanatical Japanese naval ground force (the equivalent in theory of US Marines) and the two US divisions. Massive amounts of artillery were employed to blast the Japanese out of their positions, many of them in centuries-old, earthquake-proof buildings. When the fight finally ended, over 1,000 US soldiers and, other than a few battered survivors, the entire Japanese force was dead. Manila was secure, although it would take many weeks to restore it to a level capable of supporting the future invasion of Japan. Clark Field was also secured at this time. The necessary port and airfields were now in US hands. The campaign on Luzon should have ended right there. For many thousands of US soldiers, it did not.

Even with the capture of Manila, significant Japanese forces still existed in the Philippines north of Manila and on the Bataan and Bicol Peninsulas. Bataan, which held an emotional stake in every American's mind as they thought of the brutality of the Bataan Death March, was a potential area of concern because of its close proximity to both Manila and Clark Field. It need not have been. As with all other Japanese units on Luzon, the enemy on Bataan was a stationary force, devoid of any manner of transportation or air support. US forces dominated the skies above Luzon and the waters around it. A blocking force could have easily kept the Japanese bottled up in the peninsula. Having examined MacArthur's New Guinea campaign, one could anticipate that is exactly what he would have done. When US forces landed at Hollandia in April 1944, they outflanked an entire Japanese army. When it came to the Philippines, MacArthur's strategic brilliance disappeared. Not one millimeter of Filipino territory could be left occupied by the Japanese, not a single enemy soldier could be left alive. It was at this time the Eighth Army entered the picture.

Even before MacArthur ripped units away from the Sixth Army to create the Eighth Army, US forces were at best even in strength to the enemy. The Shobu Group, responsible for Luzon north of Manila, had over 150,000 men. South of Manila was another 80,000. Five IDs and several smaller units, all of which the Sixth Army needed to liberate northern and southern Luzon (tactically and strategically unnecessary) were taken away to form the new Eighth Army. The 150,000 men in northern Luzon had no ability to attack Manila, just like those in the Bataan Peninsula. No transport, no air power. They dug into the mountains and thick jungle and allowed the Sixth Army to come to them. And come they did. Four divisions suffered in those mountains and jungle while the units that could have supported or relieved them, now forming the Eighth Army, fought to liberate islands in the Southern Philippines.

The Sixth, 25th, 32nd, and 33rd IDs spent the months after the fall of Manila flailing away in northern Luzon. The Sixth fought in the area of Wawa Dam, mistakenly believing that the dam was needed for supplying water to Manila (it was in fact the Ipo Dam that supplied that water). The division had fought hard on New Guinea and fought even harder here. Two months were spent fighting for a useless objective. When finally pulled off the line, they were no longer an effective combat unit. There were 335 dead, 1,000 wounded, and 5,000 non-battle casualties.[14] The

14 Robert Ross Smith, *Triumph In The Philippines* (Washington, DC: Center Of

non-battle casualties were victims of battle fatigue and numerous combat-induced neurological disorders, what is now referred to as post-traumatic stress disorder (PTSD). It was a little known term at the time, instead referred to as battle fatigue, and sadly many of those 5,000 would be back in action before they were provided any real help. The Sixth was not the only Army unit battered in this manner.

While the Sixth ID fought at Wawa Dam, the other units of Sixth Army began a drive north. The 32nd ID moved along the small, treacherous Villa Verde Trail, the 25th ID moved toward Balete Pass, and the 33rd ID moved toward the town of Baguio. The 32nd was the most experienced unit in MacArthur's entire command. They fought at Buna, throughout the New Guinea campaign, and on Leyte. They arrived on Luzon exhausted and understrength. The Villa Verde Trail sucked whatever they had left out of them. Fighting for various hills and passes, they faced not only the tenacious, well-entrenched Japanese, but jungles and mountains that cast aside US advantages in mobility, firepower, and airpower. Nearly three months later they finished, but the toll was high. The 32nd started the Luzon operation with 625 officers and 10,499 enlisted men. When finally pulled off the line, there were 916 dead, 2,500 wounded, and 5,000 non-battle casualties.[15] Two divisions were now off the line completely, although they would reappear in the last weeks of the war.

The 25th, a relatively fresh division when they began moving toward Balete Pass, fought in the same type of terrain as the 32nd. They suffered just as severely. The 25th had fought on Luzon since the first landings and by the time they finally stopped on May 22, had suffered 1,158 killed, 3,151 wounded, and 6,907 non-battle casualties.[16] A third division was rendered ineffective. The 33rd

---

Military History, 1963), 398.

15 32nd Infantry Division, *After Action Report, Annex #1, G-1 Report* (Headquarters: 32nd Infantry Division, 1945).

16 25th Infantry Division, *After Action Report, Medical Services Annex* (Headquarters: 25th Infantry Division, 1945), 187–89.

ID had the best terrain to fight in during their drive toward Baguio and casualties were far lighter. The whole northern Luzon operation was unnecessary. While these divisions endured, the Eighth Army fought for the islands of the Southern Philippines instead of with the Sixth Army. US units were already on Luzon, so operations there made some sense, at least tactically. The Eighth Army operations in the Southern Philippines were unjustifiable and Douglas MacArthur bears responsibility for every US soldier that died on those islands.

Once Leyte was secure, the Southern Philippines were outflanked and isolated. Each Japanese garrison on islands like Cebu and Negros was on its own, devoid of air power, support, relief, and hope. As with northern Luzon, they only entered the equation if attacked. While unnecessary, the Eighth Army operations on these islands were brilliantly executed, with several of them occurring simultaneously. Before moving into the Southern Philippines, small units of an infant Eighth Army conducted mopping-up operations on Leyte, cleared the small islands along the sea routes to Luzon, and participated in a small part of the initial drive toward Manila.

II

Compared to other US armies of WWII, the Eighth Army was relatively small, for the preponderance of its existence it never numbered more than five divisions. In only one of its operations, on Mindanao, did it even require a corps headquarters (Mindanao was the only multi-division operation undertaken by the Eighth Army). Several of its divisions had extensive combat experience. Several of its divisions went through multiple commanders. However, for command of this new army, a finer general did not exist in the Pacific than General Robert Eichelberger. By 1945, he had earned the nickname "MacArthur's Fireman" for the multiple times he had rescued stalled operations, especially at Buna and Biak. When General Krueger assumed command of Sixth Army in 1943, many most likely believed Eichelberger would receive command of the Sixth. While he made several appearances in the war under the umbrella of Sixth Army, Eichelberger waited until Leyte before receiving his first army command. As with the rest of his military career, he performed brilliantly.

Robert Eichelberger was born on March 9, 1886 in Urbana, Ohio. His military career began in 1905 when he entered the US Military Academy at West Point. He graduated in the famous class of 1909, finishing 68th out of a class of 103. The notoriety of this class derives from many of Eichelberger's fellow graduates, among them future WWII army commanders George Patton, Jacob Devers, and William Simpson. Upon graduation, Eichelberger was posted throughout the United States and at the Panama Canal. During WWI, like so many others, he was not dispatched to France and thus garnered no combat experience. But, unlike so many others, he gained fighting experience somewhere else. In Eichelberger's case, it was Siberia. His division had been earmarked for France, but was diverted to Russia, a nation in turmoil after the Communist Revolution of 1917. It was a nation that drew the scorn of the Allied powers after it withdrew from WWI. After landing at Vladivostok in August 1918, Eichelberger's division found itself fighting with the anti-communist forces in a brutal civil war. Eichelberger received the Distinguished Service Cross, the United States' second highest military award, for his service in Russia.

Major Eichelberger spent the next several years at various intelligence postings in the Philippines and China before returning to the United States during the summer of 1921. He spent the rest of the decade working at the Army General Staff's Military Intelligence Division, attending the Army's Command and General Staff and War Colleges, and in 1931 was appointed Adjutant General of West Point. By the mid-1930s he became Staff Secretary for the Army Chief of Staff, General Douglas MacArthur. A connection between the two was obviously made and fate brought them back together several years later.

In 1937, MacArthur left Washington for the Philippines to rebuild the military forces in the US territory. To achieve future high command meant serving in the infantry, which Eichelberger did as commander of the 30th Infantry Regiment at the Presidio, in San Francisco, and impressing General George Marshall, the Army Chief of Staff, which he did during several amphibious exercises in 1940. The year 1940 also saw Eichelberger's promotion to Brigadier General.[17]

Promotion brought first an appointment as Superintendent of West Point and then as commander of the 77th Infantry Division at Fort Jackson, South Carolina. The US entered WWII during

---

17 The US Army has five different levels of generals, a Brigadier General being the lowest part of the pyramid with a single star. A two star general, referred to as a Major General, typically commands a division. A three star or Lieutenant General commands either a corps or army. A General, with four stars, could command an army group or hold an extremely high political position. The final, and very rare general is a General of the Army, with five stars.

this time and Eichelberger continued to prepare his division for combat. A corps command, I Corps, was created at Fort Jackson in June 1942 and Eichelberger assumed command of the organization. Initially earmarked for *Operation Torch*, the invasion of North Africa, his corps headquarters of but a few dozen men were redirected to Australia. There they assumed command of MacArthur's first units, the 32nd and 41st Infantry Divisions. For the next several months, Eichelberger inspected the divisions and due to their obvious unpreparedness for a protracted jungle war, he instituted a strenuous training program. However, before the desired results were reached the 32nd was sent to Buna and in mid-November launched its first attack. Several weeks of failure and frustration led to MacArthur summoning Eichelberger and then dispatching him to Buna. He relieved his old West Point classmate, General Edwin Harding, and set to work rectifying a bad situation. MacArthur's Fireman was born.

It took several weeks, some new equipment, and a change of command, but by early January, Buna was in US hands.[18] Eichelberger remained in the area as commander of a combined US-Australian force cleaning up several thousand Japanese soldiers in eastern New Guinea. He then returned to Australia with his I Corps just as a new army, the Sixth, was formed. The command was given to Krueger and Eichelberger returned to training new formations. Army command was available, but the Fireman's benefactor would not allow it. Eichelberger was requested for Europe, as commander of the First Army, and then the Ninth Army. Both times MacArthur refused to let him go. Bitterly disappointed, he still poured himself into directing the first operation in New Guinea at Hollandia in April 1944.[19] Hollandia's landings were

---

18 See Chapter 6 by this author in *Bringing Order To Chaos: Historical Case Studies of Combined Arms Maneuver in Large Scale Combat Operations*, part of the US Army's Large Scale Combat Operations Series.

19 Eichelberger's frustration with the new command arrangement is clear in much of the correspondence between himself and his wife (see Jay Luvaas, *Dear Miss Em: Robert Eichelberger and the Pacific War, 1942–1945*).

unopposed. For the next few months, Eichelberger remained be-hind the scenes. In June, the Biak operation stalled. While not as overtly hopeless as Buna some 18 months earlier, MacArthur needed it to move. Coordination with Nimitz's forces depended on the use of Biak's airfields, which was impossible with Japanese forces occupying the heights. Eichelberger arrived and after a few days relieved another commander, this time 41st Infantry Divi-sion's commander General Horace Fuller. Unlike Buna, Eichel-berger needed no prodding to relieve a commander. He would fix Biak as he fixed Buna. While this happened, final preparations were made for the return to the Philippines. The landings on Leyte began on October 20, 1944 and Sixth Army controlled the fight until the end of December. The invasion of Luzon loomed and Sixth Army was needed there. Mopping up on Leyte required a new formation. That formation became the Eighth Army and the only person who could take that command in the Pacific was Robert Eichelberger.

When first entering the fight on Leyte the Eighth Army took con-trol of several Sixth Army formations to complete the "mopping up" of that island. The Eighth Army participated in the first land-ings on Luzon and the drive for Manila, its principal combat for-mation being the 11th Airborne Division. The 11th then passed back to control of the Sixth Army. Eichelberger's Eighth Army, the Americal Division and the 24th, 31st, 40th, and 41st Infan-try Divisions, then began its campaign against the islands of the Southern Philippines.

US airborne divisions, specifically the 82nd and 101st, achieved justifiable notoriety for their many remarkable exploits during the war. If one were to bring up the airborne, the focus of the dis-cussion would undoubtedly be on Europe. It's as if no airborne units even operated in the Pacific. MacArthur had an airborne division, the 11th, and though it was actively involved in the war for less than a year, it was a year of distinction. Initially, the 11th was composed of only glider units. It was first activated in February 1943 at Camp Mackall, North Carolina, and placed under the command of General Joseph Swing, the division's only commander during the war.[20] They trained in the United States and New Guinea for the next 18 months, including jump training, before actively entering the war. They landed, no airborne operation happened, on Leyte on November 18, 1944. A few weeks of organization and movement led to the division relieving several tired infantry divisions and then moving toward Ormoc, to clear a nearby mountain pass. Rock Hill, Purple Heart Hill, and several other noteworthy battles occurred during the following month, under the control of Sixth Army in which over 6,000 enemy soldiers were killed.[21] In mid-January 1945, the 11th Airborne was pulled off the line to rest and refit.[22] It was a short rest, only a week. The 11th Airborne Division was transferred to the Eighth Army for the first landings on Luzon.

Of the five infantry divisions that made up Eighth Army, several had extensive combat experience. The Americal Division was one such unit. The division was initially activated under the command of General Alexander Patch.[23] The Americal seemed to have a revolving door of commanders. In addition to Patch, the division commanders for the duration of the war were as follows:

General Edmund Seabree (January–May 1943)

General John Hodge (May 1943–April 1944)

General Robert McClure (April–October 1944)

General William Arnold (November 1944–end of war)[24]

---

20 Edward Flanagan, *The Angels: A History Of The 11ᵗʰ Airborne Division, 1943–1946* (Washington, DC: Infantry Journal Press, 1948), 1.

21 *Ibid.,* 62.

22 *Ibid.*

23 Francis Cronin, *Under the Southern Cross: The Saga of the Americal Division* (Washington, DC: Combat Forces Press, 1951), 27.

24 *World War II Division Combat Chronicles, Americal Division,* https://history. army.mil.

The division first entered the war on October 13, 1942, on Guadalcanal, the first US Army unit to conduct any active offensive operation against the enemy in WWII. It was involved in three major operations. The first was assisting the First Marine Division in its defense of Henderson Field, the whole purpose of the invasion of Guadalcanal. They were major participants in the Battle of Tassafaronga, along the Matanikau River. They also launched a major attack against Mount Austen on December 17.[25] The campaign followed a pattern of attacks in thick jungle and debilitating heat, defending against Japanese infiltration efforts and night attacks, and constant patrols. The division remained on Guadalcanal until its relief in February.[26] It was a costly operation for the division's baptism of fire. A total of 354 men were killed and nearly 1,000 were wounded in the division's three months of action.[27] From Guadalcanal, the American moved to the Fiji Islands, where it spent the remainder of 1943 training for future operations. On Christmas Day, the division moved to the island of Bougainville.

The American remained on Bougainville until the end of November 1944. They relieved the Third Marine Division and initially were content with holding the established perimeter. Over the next months, they extended their perimeter, conducted vigorous patrolling, and trained. Relieved at the end of 1944, the American moved to Leyte where it was one of several divisions involved in the "mopping up" of the island. While on Leyte, it joined the newly formed Eighth Army.

Another formation within Eighth Army was the 24th Infantry Division. It participated in the war the moment Pearl Harbor was attacked, as the division was stationed at Schofield Barracks on Oahu. The 24th remained on Oahu until May 1943 when they were ordered to Australia.[28] The division trained until they

25 Richard Frank, *Guadalcanal* (New York: Penguin Books, 1990), 530–31.

26 Cronin, *Under the Southern Cross*, 70.

27 Frank, *Guadalcanal*, 764.

28 *World War II Division Combat Chronicles, 24th Infantry Division*, https://history.army.mil.

participated in the Hollandia landings. Most of the division remained at Hollandia throughout the summer of 1944. One of its regiments, the 34th Infantry Regiment, deployed to Biak. At this time, the division was on its second commander, General Frederick Irving, who replaced first commander, General Durward Wilson, in August 1942.[29] The 34th fought in the dense coral and caves of Biak for several weeks before returning to division control at Hollandia. The 24th remained on New Guinea, continually training, until October 20, 1944, when it landed on Leyte with the rest of Sixth Army.

Leyte was a vicious, costly fight for the 24th ID. A total of 544 were killed in action and another 1,784 were wounded during the campaign; many more succumbed to fatigue and heat.[30] Of its many battles on Leyte, the Battle of Breakneck Ridge achieved the most notoriety, both for its name and ferocity. Fighter-bombers, artillery, tanks, and infantry assault teams (equipped with explosives, bazookas, and flamethrowers) dealt with mud, torrential rains, and a tenacious, dug-in enemy. One of the division's infantry regiments, the 21st, killed 1,779 Japanese soldiers at the cost of 630 killed, wounded, and missing.[31] Another 135 men were non-battle casualties.[32] The 21st lost nearly half its strength in this battle and under ordinary circumstances would need several months to recover. That time wasn't available. The division moved to Mindoro in December to prepare for its anticipated landing on Luzon, which happened on January 29, 1945.

For the 24th Infantry Division Breakneck Ridge symbolized its fight on Leyte. On Luzon it was Zig Zag Pass. The division also had its third wartime commander on Luzon, General Roscoe Woodruff, who replaced General Irving in November 1944. It

---

29 Ibid.

30 M. Hamlin Cannon, Leyte: The Return To The Philippines (Washington, DC: Center Of Military History, 1954), 368.

31 Ibid., 220.

32 Ibid.

was another vicious, protracted fight on ground. The Army's official campaign historian, Robert Ross Smith, noted: "While more rugged terrain than the Zig Zag Pass area is to be found on Luzon, few pieces of ground combine to the same degree both roughness and dense jungle."[33] Several days of heavy fighting against well-prepared enemy defenses by both the 24th and 38th IDs accomplished little other than heavy US casualties. It was eventually secured; every objective sought by the US military at this point of the war was eventually secured. It was just a matter of necessity, time, and cost. A battalion of the 24th also fought on Corregidor, the small island in Manila Bay referred to as the "Rock." The division was then pulled off the line, transferred from Sixth to Eighth Army, and awaited its next mission.

Two of the other divisions joining Eighth Army did not have the extensive combat experience of the American and 24th Infantry Divisions. The 31st and 40th Infantry Divisions were both created from conglomerates of National Guard units, the 31st from the Southeast, and the 40th from the West. The 31st was under the command of General John Persons from the time of its activation in November 1940 through September 1944.[34] General Clarence Martin then commanded the division for the duration of the war. The division trained in the United States before arriving in New Guinea after the Hollandia landings. One of its regiments, the 124th, participated in the covering force operation during the summer of 1944 along the Drinumor River, conducting reconnaissance and active patrolling. The division as a whole engaged sporadic Japanese forces until mid-September, when they landed on the island of Morotai, meeting only an occasional Japanese straggler or patrol.[35] The division continued training until the spring of 1945 when they joined the Eighth Army.

33 Smith, *Triumph In The Philippines*, 315.

34 *World War II Division Combat Chronicles, 31st Infantry Division*, https://history.army.mil.

35 *Ibid.*

The 40th Infantry Division also saw little action before the invasion of Luzon. Other than a few months at the beginning of the war, General Rapp Brush commanded the division. From the fall of 1942 until the end of 1943 the 40th maintained the defense of Hawaii. The year 1944 saw the division on Guadalcanal and New Britain, seeing no major action.[36] The division landed with other Sixth Army units on Luzon at Lingayen Gulf on January 9, 1945. The 40th began advancing toward Manila, fighting protracted battles in the Fort Stotsenburg area and in the Bambam Hills.[37] In March, the 40th Infantry Division was transferred from the control of Sixth to Eighth Army.

The last of the major formations of the Eighth Army was the 41st Infantry Division, along with the 32nd Infantry Division, the longest serving unit of MacArthur's command. The division had two wartime commanders: General Horace Fuller and Jens Doe. Fuller commanded the division from the war's start to Biak, where General Eichelberger relieved him. General Doe then led the division for the remainder of the war. The 41st first arrived in Australia in April 1942 and trained there until arriving at the end of Buna operation.[38] Throughout 1943, the division split its time between New Guinea and Australia, patrolling and training. It landed with other Sixth Army units at Hollandia before conducting one of the war's textbook operations on the small island of Wakde. From Wakde, the 41st moved to an invasion of Biak. Biak was many things; a textbook operation is not one of them. An inability to clear the heights overlooking the island's vital airfields led to the relief of General Fuller and General Doe's assumption of command. Over the next several weeks Biak was cleared and secured. The 41st remained on New Guinea until February 1945,

---

36 *World War II Division Combat Chronicles, 40th Infantry Division,* https://history.army.mil.

37 *Ibid.*

38 *World War II Division Combat Chronicles, 41st Infantry Division,* https://history.army.mil.

when it landed in the Philippines at Mindoro. It then passed to the Eighth Army.

Other units joined the Eighth Army in July 1945, when it assumed control of the "mopping up" portion of the Luzon operation. Many Filipino guerrilla units and the 37th Infantry Division came under their control. The Sixth Army was pulled back to prepare for the invasion of Japan, an invasion that never happened. With each of the operations to be discussed in the following pages, some time will be dedicated to the Filipino Guerrilla Force, a force that while generally not decisive, did play a role in the eventual defeat of the Japanese.

III

Heartiest Congratulations on capture of Palompon. This closes a campaign that has had few counterparts in the utter destruction of the enemy's forces with a maximum conservation of our own. It has been a magnificent performance on the part of all concerned.

—General Douglas MacArthur
to General Walter Krueger[39]

On December 26, 1944, General Eichelberger received a late Christmas present. The Eighth Army was activated and he assumed control of the "mopping up" phase of the Leyte operation. The above message was sent by General MacArthur on Christmas day. Its congratulatory nature makes it seem as if the campaign was over. It was not. As the Army's official historian of the campaign noted: "The mop-up of any operation is dangerous, difficult, and unglamorous, but it is highly essential."[40] Public perception, at least among the military hierarchy, may have been that this would be an easy fight. Considering the Eighth Army killed over one-third of the total enemy dead on the island, that perception is far from reality.[41]

If one were to accept Sixth Army estimates of remaining Japanese strength on Leyte, Eichelberger's men could have expected a relatively easy fight. The Sixth Army informed Eichelberger that only 5,000 Japanese soldiers remained on Leyte and the nearby island

39 M. Hamlin Cannon, *Leyte,* 361.

40 *Ibid.,* 365.

41 Eighth Army, *Report Of The Commanding General Eighth US Army On The Leyte-Samar Operation (Including Clearance of the Visayan Passages), 26 December 1944–8 May 1945* (Headquarters: Eighth Army, 1945), 9.

of Samar.[42] That would have been easy work for the units that the Eighth Army assumed control of for the "mopping up" portion of the Leyte campaign. Eichelberger commanded the 11th Airborne Division and the Seventh, 77th, and 96th Infantry Divisions. His units had participated in the campaign and were understandably tired and with the exception of the 11th Airborne, the infantry divisions were moving to Tenth Army, where they joined the invasion of Okinawa. They also knew what still awaited them on Leyte and it was not only 5,000 Japanese soldiers.[43] Over the next five months, the last action on Leyte was May 8, 1945, the Eighth Army accounted for over 25,000 enemy dead. Few knew about these numbers, least of all General MacArthur. Once he declared a campaign closed, his interest in it disappeared. The Eighth Army's actions on Leyte are not mentioned in MacArthur's *Reminiscences* or his WWII Operational Reports, nor are they mentioned in the memoirs of those who served on MacArthur's staff.[44] The "Forgotten" Eighth Army was born on Leyte.

The Eighth Army's mission on Leyte was outlined in its December 20, 1944 Field Order No. 8, stating: "the XXIV Corps to continue the destruction of Japanese wherever found and to be prepared to conduct overland or amphibious shore-to-shore operations to seize enemy supply points, bases, and points of entry."[45] The Army's official volumes of WWII are excellent works, essentially primary sources written in the years immediately after the war. Writers were given full access to operational records, prisoner interrogations, and US participants. M. Hamlin Cannon

---

42 *Ibid.,* 3.

43 *Ibid.*

44 Two members of MacArthur's staff, General Charles Willoughby and John Chamberlain, wrote a book titled *MacArthur: 1941–1951*. It was a blatant fluff piece that never even mentioned the Eighth Army. MacArthur's Chief of Staff, General Richard Sutherland, wrote an equally useless work, *The Good Years: MacArthur and Sutherland.*

45 Eighth Army, *Report Of The Commanding General Eighth US Army On The Leyte-Samar Operation (Including Clearance of the Visayan Passages), 26 December 1944–8 May 1945,* 7.

wrote the Leyte edition, *Leyte: The Return To The Philippines.* It is an outstanding work of 370 pages, but the "mopping up" portion of this vast volume is but three paragraphs. Cannon wrote:

> the 11th Airborne Division encountered an enemy force well dug in on the southern slopes of Mt. Majunag, five miles northwest of Burauen. After much bitter hand-to-hand fighting the Japanese were destroyed. The 96th Division engaged in extensive patrolling, relieved the 11th Airborne Division, and relieved the X Corps of all tactical responsibility east of the mountains. The 7th Division sent out numerous patrols in the southern part of the island, and sent out a reinforced battalion that destroyed all enemy forces in the Camotes Islands. The 77th Division, which operated in the northwestern part of the island, cleared up many pockets of enemy resistance.[46]

That's it. A few paragraphs for 25,000 enemy dead. General Eichelberger actually estimated enemy dead a bit higher, at over 27,000.[47] The Eighth Army losses weren't minimal. "Mopping up" resulted in 432 killed, 1,852 wounded, and 22 missing.[48]

As the synopsis of the Eighth Army proceeds, a potential asset for US ground forces, Filipino guerillas, will be repeatedly addressed. On the islands of the Philippines where the Eighth Army operated, mostly isolated enemy garrisons on vast lands, guerillas had an opportunity to make an important impact. In some cases they were helpful; in others they were not. Regardless of effectiveness,

---

46 Canon, *Leyte: The Return To The Philippines,* 365.

47 Robert L. Eichelberger, *Our Jungle Road To Tokyo* (New York: The Viking Press, 1950), 181.

48 Eighth Army, *Report Of The Commanding General Eighth US Army On The Leyte-Samar Operation (Including Clearance of the Visayan Passages), 26 December 1944–8 May 1945,* 16.

Filipino guerillas had to be taken into account, by both the Americans and the Japanese.

On Leyte, the guerilla movement began soon after the Japanese landed and took control of the island.[49] For nearly three years, several different groups operated on the island, uncoordinated, and of little military effectiveness. Until US troops landed in October 1944, the Japanese still dominated Leyte. The island's total number of guerillas was 3,190.[50] They became actively involved in the "mopping up" phase of the operation entrusted to the Eighth Army. They pinpointed hidden Japanese detachments, supply points, and local command centers, positions for which a local populace would have direct knowledge. They did not play a decisive role in the campaign, but definitely helped.

On Leyte, the 11th Airborne Division was only involved in Eighth Army operations for four days (December 26–29). They returned to the Eighth Army a few weeks later, as the main force In Eichelberger's limited involvement in the Luzon operation. During those four days, they finished up a battle on the slopes of Mt. Majunag.[51] It was a vicious fight in the holes the Japanese dug into the mountains and jungle. For the 11th, it may have been an even tougher fight than for the infantry divisions of both the Sixth and Eighth Armies. Airborne divisions during WWII were far weaker than their infantry counterparts in both numbers and equipment. The 11th had two glider and one parachute infantry regiments. All three of those regiments had far less rifleman than a standard infantry regiment, resulting in a total strength of 8,200 men, as compared to the 16,000–17,000 men in a standard infantry division.[52] Their artillery was 75-mm pack howitzers, limited

---

49 *The Guerilla Resistance Movement In The Philippines* (General Headquarters: United States Army Forces, Pacific Military Intelligence Section, General Staff, 1945), 1.

50 *Ibid.*, 4.

51 XXIV Corps, *Operations Report: XXIV Corps, Leyte, 26 December 1944 – 10 February 1945* (Headquarters: XXIV Corps, 1945), 4.

52 Smith, 223.

in range and effectiveness. There were no tanks or self-propelled guns. An airborne division's greatest asset was speed and mobility. Those assets work fabulously until caught in a protracted fight against a well-entrenched enemy. The Japanese were that enemy. The 11th Airborne Division won, but it was a hard fight.

The 96th Infantry Division also passed to Eighth Army control during this time. It spent this period actively patrolling and relieving other active Leyte units, such as the 11th and the remnants of X Corps.[53] One of its regiments was also detached to the island of Samar, relieving troops in garrison there. The Eighth Army' other Leyte formations, the 77th and Seventh Infantry Divisions were more active though still engaged in "mopping up."

The 77th Infantry Division was given the mission by the Eighth Army of "securing the Liburgac-Palompon Highway and capturing the last Japanese escape port of Pamompon."[54] The division had several bloody battles in the following weeks, one of those against a position known as the "blockhouse," a three-story stone and concrete building surrounded by pillboxes and foxholes.[55] The fire of three artillery battalions (over 50 105-mm guns), self-propelled howitzers (a dozen 105-mm guns), M-10 tank destroyers (a dozen 75-mm guns), mortars, machine guns, and everything else the infantry could throw in the fight hit the "blockhouse."[56] For several days, every attack was thrown back by the Japanese until infantry and tank destroyers were able to advance to within feet of the enemy. Victory came with over 800 enemy dead.[57]

---

53 XXIV Corps, *Operations Report: XXIV Corps, Leyte, 26 December 1944–10 February 1945*, 4.

54 305th Infantry Regiment, *A/A RPT – Leyte Campaign – 305th Infantry Regiment, 77th Infantry Division, 26 December 44–2 February 45* (Headquarters: 305th Infantry Regiment, 1945), 1.

55 *Ibid.,* 3.

56 *Ibid.,* 4.

57 *Ibid.,* 7.

Most of the fighting involving the 77th was not as protracted as that for the "blockhouse." By the end of 1944, the organized defense of Leyte by the Japanese was broken. However, there were still substantial numbers of enemy soldiers on the island, a point reinforced by the over 25,000 Japanese killed by Eighth Army before the end of the war. Those enemy soldiers had to be located which meant patrolling and pursuit. One of the 77th's regiments, the 305th Infantry Regiment, spent the month of January 1945 patrolling and pursuing that elusive enemy. Below demonstrates how successful they were:

DATE	TYPE OF ACTION	JAPANESE LOSSES
January 2	Patrolling/Movement to Contact	18 KIA
January 4	Patrolling/Movement to Contact	10 KIA
January 5	Patrolling/Movement to Contact	4 KIA
January 8	Patrolling/Movement to Contact	4 KIA
January 9	Patrolling/Movement to Contact	32 KIA
January 10	Patrolling/Movement to Contact	85 KIA
January 11	Patrolling/Movement to Contact	24 KIA
January 12	Conventional Attack	43 KIA
January 13	Conventional Attack	146 KIA
January 14	Conventional Attack	140 KIA
January 15	Japanese Counterattack	388 KIA
January 16	Japanese Counterattack	133 KIA
January 17	Patrolling	39 KIA
January 18	Patrolling	52 KIA
January 19	Patrolling	26 KIA
January 20	Patrolling	20 KIA
January 21	Japanese Probing	17 KIA
January 23	Patrolling	2 KIA
January 24	Patrolling	8 KIA
January 25	Patrolling	39 KIA
January 27	Patrolling	10 KIA
January 29	Japanese Probing	99 KIA
January 30	Conventional Attack	41 KIA
January 31	Conventional Attack	56 KIA[58]

---

58 *Ibid.,* 10–20.

One month of action cost the Japanese dearly. For the 305th, it cost 42 dead and 113 wounded.[59]

The Seventh Infantry Division was the last of the major Eighth Army units involved in "mopping up" Leyte. As pointed out by the Seventh's official history of the campaign:

> Division operations during the mopping up period were based on the ruined town of Ormoc, lying on the west coast of Leyte at the head of Ormoc Bay. From this port, the Ormoc Corridor, a swampy and roughly cultivated valley, extends north northeast toward Carigara Bay. It is bordered on the east by rugged heavily overgrown mountains on the main Leyte Watershed, and on the West by a lower, parallel mountain chain which extends north to Rabin Point and south to the tip of Leyte Peninsula. The Division MSR (Main Supply Route) from Ormoc to Baybay followed the shoreline closely and traversed a narrow coastal plain.[60]

Within the Seventh's area of responsibility were approximately 6,000 Japanese soldiers.[61] There was no cohesion whatsoever to those 6,000 troops. They were scattered about and had to be found through extensive patrolling:

> the Division operated an average of 30 patrols daily in addition to major troop movements. At no time, did the enemy maintain an organized line of resistance, and for the most part, sought to avoid combat. The period was characterized by small engagements, which in conjunction

---

59 *Ibid.*

60 Seventh Infantry Division, *Operations Report: 7th Infantry Division, King II*, 22 (Headquarters: Seventh Infantry Division, 1945).

61 *Ibid.*, 22–23.

with disease and starvation, reduced enemy forces day by day. A high percentage of patrols were accompanied by artillery forward observation parties, and maximum use made of supporting arms.[62]

A typical engagement occurred near Canale. A group of enemy soldiers, 45 men, were eliminated by artillery fire called in by one of those parties of forward observers.[63] An enemy position along the Ormoc-Canale trail stubbornly defended by several dozen men was overrun by tanks and infantry. Advances continued and many days saw little or no enemy contact while others a random Japanese force. The Seventh's month of January essentially mirrored that of the 77th, though the Seventh eliminated more Japanese soldiers with artillery fire than direct action. Patrolling was the main method used to locate the Japanese, although the island's guerillas also played a role. Unfortunately, exact locations of enemy troops and their strength were not accurate, with the division history noting: "Estimates of enemy strength were the most inaccurate of civilian reports, and reports given by guerilla officers were often grossly exaggerated."[64] They were helpful as interrogators, but as with most operations in the Philippines, their value was not decisive.

The Seventh Infantry Division finished its campaign on Leyte on February 10, 1945. They killed 16,559 Japanese soldiers and took 233 prisoners while suffering losses of 582 killed and 2,102 wounded.[65] The majority of those losses happened before the Seventh joined the Eighth Army. Mopping up continued on Leyte, under Eighth Army control, by various scattered units un-

---

62 *Ibid.,* 23.

63 *Ibid.*

64 Seventh Infantry Division, *Operations Report: 7th Infantry Division, King II, Intelligence Annex* (Headquarters: Seventh Infantry Division, 1945), 1.

65 Seventh Infantry Division, *Operations Report: 7th Infantry Division, King II,* 34.

til May, but by February 1945, Eichelberger and his staff shifted their focus to Luzon. For a short period of time, the Eighth Army participated in the drive to Manila.

After Leyte, the Eighth Army joined Sixth Army for the early days of the Luzon campaign. First, the Eighth had to clear the Visayan Passages, the narrow sea-lanes leading from Leyte through the Southern Philippines to Luzon. The mission was dictated by a February letter sent from MacArthur to General Eichelberger: "Eighth Army institute operations at the earliest practicable date to clear the northern coast of Samar and the islands in the Cape Verde Passage with the objective of securing the southern exits to San Bernardino Straits and Verde Island Passage."[66] The operations were relatively simple and enemy opposition negligible. On the islands of the San Bernardino Strait (Capul, Biri, and Pauo Town on northern Samar), there were less than 1,000 total Japanese soldiers.[67] By February 26, all San Bernardino islands were clear of the Japanese. The Verde Island Passage saw some fighting, resulting in 82 enemy dead, three prisoners, and six wounded Americans.[68] It was fast and easy, and MacArthur flooded Eichelberger and the Eighth Army with praise. One such message stated: "My heartiest commendations for the brilliant execution of the Visayan Campaign. This is a model of what a light but aggressive command can accomplish in rapid exploitation."[69] This message was at the end of February, and it seems by tone and semantics that MacArthur considered the campaign over. It was not, but such a declaration by the Southwest Pacific Area's commander was neither uncommon nor unexpected. He had done so at Buna and Biak, at Leyte, and continued to do so throughout the

---

66 Eighth Army, *Report Of The Commanding General Eighth US Army On The Leyte-Samar Operation (Including Clearance of the Visayan Passages), 26 December 1944–8 May 1945,* 20.

67 *Ibid.,* 24.

68 *Ibid.*

69 Eichelberger, *Our Jungle Road To Tokyo,* 193.

fight on Luzon. General Eichelberger actually stated as much in his post-war memoir: "I must admit that after serving under him for over six years I never understood the public relations policy that either he or his immediate assistants established. It seemed to me, as it did to many of the commanders and correspondents, ill advised to announce victories when a first phase had been accomplished without too many casualties."[70] There was still work to be done. In March, elements of the Eighth Army landed in the Lubang Island Group, on Ticao and Burias islands, and several islands centrally located between Mindoro and Masbate. Enemy casualties were heavy, US casualties light. Unlike Leyte, Filipino guerillas played a more positive role. Japanese numbers were still exaggerated, but enemy locations were accurate and the guerillas served as guides and garrisoned the islands after US forces departed.[71] Luzon was next and had far more Japanese forces than the Visayan Passages.

On January 31, 1945 the 11th Airborne Division landed on Luzon. The Sixth Army landed at Lingayen Gulf, on Luzon's western coast, north of Manila. The 11th, the sole Eighth Army representative in this operation, landed at Naugbu Bay, south of Manila. The Sixth Army drove south toward the city while the 11th rushed north. Yet, Manila was not even mentioned as an objective for Eighth Army.[72] The 11th's original mission was essentially a reconnaissance in force, hoping to block fleeing Japanese moving south

---

70 *Ibid.*, 176.

71 Eighth Army, *Report Of The Commanding General Eighth US Army On The Leyte-Samar Operation (Including Clearance of the Visayan Passages), 26 December 1944–8 May 1945*, 31.

72 Flanagan, *The Angels*, 67.

When it comes to records for the 11th Airborne Division, the options are few. All of the division's official records were destroyed in Japan after the war. Colonel Flanagan's work is a primary source as he was a member of the division during the war. It is very positive throughout the book, which, given his participation in the unit, is not surprising. Robert Ross Smith's official history of the Luzon campaign and Cannon's work on Leyte are the only other sources that have much value.

from the advancing Sixth Army.[73] The landing of initially a single regiment was easy and devoid of most opposition, as the Japanese at this stage of the war preferred to fight inland. The second glider regiment then landed to exploit an opportunity offered by the lack of enemy opposition. The first possible obstacle was a bridge.

The Palico River Bridge traversed a 250-foot wide and 85-foot deep gorge on the fastest route to Tagaytay Ridge, the Eighth Army's first major objective.[74] Should the Japanese destroy the bridge, the 11th would have to involve itself in the type of close quarter fighting for which it had neither the men nor equipment. Speed solved the problem. The advance from the beachhead was so rapid that the Japanese did not have the time to ignite the demolitions they prepared on the bridge and the division captured it completely intact.[75] Once past the bridge, the 11th traveled through typical Filipino terrain, plenty of mountains with thick jungle everywhere. The division had to stay on the road, Highway 17, or become bogged down. By the end of that first day, the Japanese were retreating in confusion. Such an easy advance did not continue, as the division met a significant Japanese position at Mt. Aiming, near Butulao and Carilao. Bunkers, trenches, tank traps, and plentiful artillery awaited the 11th on Day 2 of the operation, February 1.

While lacking heavy artillery and tanks, the 11th could count on heavy air support from the US Fifth Air Force. Fighters and attack planes hit the Japanese position and by noon, Mt. Aiming itself was secure. The advance continued and a hard truth faced the airborne: they were incredibly outnumbered. The division's historian noted:

> On Luzon south of Manila G-2 reports claimed the presence of at least 50,000 Japs. We had

---

73 *Ibid.*

74 Smith, 225.

75 Flanagan, 71.

about 7,800 men including port details, service units, and men in hospital. We were pulling the supreme bluff. By roaring down the road, raising a lot of dust, moving in fast and shooting quickly, we left the Japs with the impression that an army complete with an armored division was making an invasion in force against them on Southern Luzon. Instead, the invading task force was a small, light airborne division, understrength and even under-manned. Replacements for our Leyte losses had not been received.[76]

Japanese numbers were formidable, as were the positions they occupied. Though Mt. Aiming was in the 11th's hands more enemy positions in the Cariliao-Batulao area remained. The division artillery and air attacks preceded a February 2 attack and eventually most of the Japanese artillery positions were eliminated.[77]

The 11th Airborne Division had fought those first days with another disadvantage: they did not have all their units yet on Luzon. The 511th Parachute Infantry Regiment was still on Leyte, but arrived on February 3 and 4 in multiple jumps, although they were unable to bring their artillery due to a shortage of transport planes. Tagaytay Ridge, the division's initial strategic objective, was attacked on February 3. Forty 75-mm pack howitzers hit the ridge but had little effect. The ridge had numerous caves and tunnels, so air attacks did little damage. The infantry did the work. Cave by cave, tunnel by tunnel, and hole by hole, they eliminated the enemy. By the afternoon, the ridge was secure and the next phase of the operation, a dash for Manila, began. In less than 96 hours, the speed of the division advance produced a major victory. The dash continued on foot for most, but the 511th got many

---

76 *Ibid.*, 73.

77 *Ibid.*, 74.

of its men on newly arrived trucks and a true high-speed advance proceeded.[78]

So impressive were these few days by the 11th that General Eichelberger awarded the division a Distinguished Unit Citation, which stated:

> The 11th Airborne Division is cited for out-standing heroism and superior performance of duty in action against the enemy on Luzon, Philippine Islands. On 31 January 1945 the 11th Airborne Division landed on the southern coast of Luzon at Nasugbu which had been or-ganized for defense by the enemy during their three years of occupation. By determined and aggressive action, employing only infantry with light artillery support, the town of Nasugbu was seized and a spearhead pushed rapidly to the east. By speed and maneuver, through forced marches over extremely difficult terrain, the de-files on the approaches to Tagaytay Ridge were captured one day after landing. Tagaytay Ridge and the avenues of approach to Cavite Plains were seized by the third day. On the fourth day, the town of Imus was by-passed, a bridgehead was established across the Paranaque River and the enemy were driven from their main defen-sive positions south of Nichols Field. The rapid progress of the division, made possible through by-passing strong points and using a minimum of troops for the reduction of obstacles, com-pletely disrupted the enemy strategy of defense. In the period of four days, the 11th Airborne Division in marching and fighting their way through sixty miles of enemy-held territory and

---

78 *Ibid.*, 75–77.

maintaining an undefended line of communication completely disorganized the enemy forces, weakening them in the north and thereby hastening the fall of Manila.[79]

Well-deserved praise for a first class division from the army commander. By nightfall on February 4, the division was at the foot of the Paranaque River Bridge, on Manila's doorstep, and a key position on the Japanese Genko Line.

The Genko Line:

> consisted of a series of concrete pillboxes, mutually supporting, and extending in depth six thousand yards through the Manila Polo Club. It stretched east across Nichols Field and anchored on the high ground of Fort McKinley. Five and six inch guns and 150mm mortars were set in concrete emplacements, facing south, and 20-, 40-, and 90-mm antiaircraft guns were strategically situated to assist in the ground defenses. Many of the concrete pillboxes were two and three stories deep .... Some of the forts were stone and had dome-shaped roofs piled high with sod and soggy dirt and so grown over with a tangle of weeds that they could be reorganized only a few feet away .... Most of the pillboxes were defended by two men and either a .50 caliber machine gun or a 20mm automatic weapon. Some positions were occupied by only one Jap, who stayed at his post until he was killed.

> .... In the Genko Line the enemy occupied over 1,200 pillboxes and generally defended each one to the last occupant.. The Japs employed

---

44 heavy artillery pieces, 164 antiaircraft 20- to 40mm guns, and a great number of machine guns, of which 333 were captured or destroyed by us during the period 5-23 February. The belt of concrete and steel was further reinforced with 245 100-pound bombs, and 35 antisubmarine depth charges, emplaced and rigged as land mines. All roads approaching the line were heavily mined with 500-pound aerial bombs armed with low-pressure detonators. This was what the Angels, lightly equipped, were up against. Our heaviest artillery was the sawed off 105.[80]

For the next 16 days, the outnumbered, lightly armed troopers of the 11th Airborne fought against these formidable defenses. US losses were high, but the 11th accounted for 5,210 dead enemy soldiers.[81] That ended the Eighth Army's role in the Luzon campaign. The bypassed islands of the Southern Philippines were the new objective. This objective also saw the transfer of the 11th Airborne from the Eighth to the Sixth Army. The first of these operations occurred on the island of Palawan and the Zamboanga Peninsula on southern Mindanao.

---

80 Flanagan, 82–83.

81 *Ibid.,* 84.

IV

After the failure of Japanese mines on Blowout Hill began the phase of hill fighting. No one in the Regiment will ever forget the outpouring of Filipino refugees who had been trapped between our shellfire and the desperate Japanese. Some had been held as hostages. They told tales of murder and rape and mutilation by Japanese. Even children displayed pus-filled bolo scars. The men of the 163rd saw, concretely, as they could not in the New Guinea wilderness, all that they were fighting for.[82]

—163rd Infantry Regiment,
41st Infantry Division

When the Eighth Army began its operations in the Southern Philippines, the targets were the island of Palawan and the Zamboanga Peninsula on the Philippines second largest island, Mindanao. The operations were polar opposites of each other. Palawan was simple. It contained a small Japanese garrison and US casualties were very light. Zamboanga was far more difficult. The terrain was mostly rugged mountains, the Japanese force larger and better supplied than that on Palawan, and US casualties were substantially higher. Both operations fell to the 41st Infantry Division.

Palawan was first. Only 1,750 Japanese troops, of which only a few hundred were combat troops, garrisoned Palawan.[83] The 41st's 186th Regimental Combat Team had over 8,000 men.[84] In-

---

82   163rd Infantry Regiment, *Historical Report: V-4 Operation: Zamboanga* (Headquarters: 163rd Infantry Regiment, 1945), 1.

83   Smith, 589.

84   *Ibid.*

formation on Japanese strength and dispositions came primarily from the active guerrilla network on the island. As major US forces fought on Luzon, why would a militarily insignificant island be the focus of a major operation? As noted in the Eighth Army report on Palawan:

> In the PALAWAN GROUP, two major and several minor sites are available for naval bases. CORON BAY in the CALAMIANES and MALAMPAYA SOUND in northwest PALAWAN are both suitable to meet the requirements of major advanced fleet bases, while PUERTO PRINCESA BAY (a naval base under Spanish rule and the primary objective of the Victor-III Operation), ULUGAN BAY, HALSEY HARBOR, PORT ZEB PETERS, and others are considered adequate for development into various types of subsidiary bases.[85]

In all operations under MacArthur's direction, directly or in this case indirectly, a future objective existed. Here, it was not support for operations on Luzon, where the Sixth Army plodded along in rugged mountains and thick jungle, but for the eventual invasion of the main islands of Japan. MacArthur wanted to return to the Philippines, for his own honor and that of his nation. But Japan itself was the prize.

The first landings on Palawan occurred on February 28, 1945. They were unopposed and the airstrips, along with Puerto Princess Bay and any other significant objectives were quickly secured. The small Japanese Palawan force moved away from the beaches and dug into the hills overlooking Puerto Princess. A few weeks of sporadic fighting, heavy at times, resulted in 11 Americans killed and 40 wounded by the time fighting ended on March

---

85   Eighth Army, *Report of the Commanding General Eighth Army on the Palawan and Zamboanga Operation* (Headquarters: Eighth Army, 1945), 4.

28.[86] Japanese losses were 890 killed and 20 prisoners.[87] The remainder of the enemy garrison scattered throughout the island, electing to stay hidden while trying to survive. They remained there until the end of the war. While securing the island, US forces found evidence of Japanese barbarism, something that became all too common as more Filipino territory was liberated. At Puerto Princess, US troops found:

> an example of one of the most cruel and barbaric atrocities ever committed by any nation. About 150 prisoners, who had been captured by the Japanese in the early stages of the war, had been confined there and used as labor gangs. In late 1944 when the Allied noose began to tighten around the enemy's throat the prisoners were herded into two air-raid shelters, which were soaked with gasoline and ignited. Those attempting to escape were mowed down with machine guns. Only four men managed to survive this ordeal by breaking through the end of a tunnel which led to the open face of a cliff over-looking the sea.[88]

Unfortunately, this was not a unique event. Japanese war crimes occurred throughout the Southern Philippines.

Unfortunately, the above was not the only example of brutality against US prisoners. Another such example occurred on Palawan at a camp in Puerto Princess. The US prisoners were forced to build an airfield. While this happened, several prisoners either escaped or attempted to escape. The Japanese responded to these attempts by:

---

86   William F. McCartney, *The Jungleers: A History of the 41st Infantry Division* (Washington, DC: The 41st Infantry Division Association, 1948).

87   *Ibid.*

88   *Ibid.*

1. Placing all prisoners on one-third rations

2. Breaking the arm of a prisoner who refused to concede inferiority

3. Tied escapees to a coconut tree in the center of the compund, beat them with wire whips and poles until unconscious, revived, and then continuously tortured them

4. One or two men were beaten in the same manner as #3 each day

5. An appendectomy was performed on a prisoner without anesthesia

6. An escaped prisoner was decapitated and his head placed on a pole in the center of the compound as a warning to all others.[89]

The above were part of a continuous ordeal faced by US prisoners, not just on Palawan, but throughout the Philippines. However, an even more sinister, murderous plot by the Japanese was devised as the war clearly fell out of their favor.

In 1944, US air raids throughout the Philippines became more common as the momentum built toward the eventual return at Leyte in October of that year. The Japanese "seemed to take the attitude that the prisoners were the cause of the bombings and treatment became worse."[90] The Japanese, supposedly to protect the US prisoners, had the prisoners build a deep air raid shelter, with only one entrance. The Japanese:

> informed the men while in barracks that they were going to work early the next morning (15 December 1944). So, they began at dawn but

---

89 Theater Judge Advocate, *Atrocities at Puerto Princess, Palawan* (General Headquarters: United States Army Forces, Pacific, Office Of The Theater Judge Advocate, War Crimes Branch, 1945), 2–4.

90 *Ibid.,* 4.

were called back at noon, which caused the Americans to sense something strange. There were two air raids during lunch and extra guards were placed around the compound. During the early afternoon another air raid warning was sounded and the men were forced into the shelter and required to remain under cover, the Japs saying that there were hundreds of American planes approaching. When everyone was securely below the ground, between 50 and 60 Jap soldiers, armed with light machine guns, rifles and carrying buckets of gasoline, attacked the unsuspecting, defenseless prisoners in the first shelter where there were approximately 40 men. They first threw a lighted torch into the entrance and followed it with a bucket or two of gasoline which exploded, setting everyone within on fire. As screaming men ran from the shelter, they were mowed down by machine guns and rifles while others, realizing they were trapped, ran to the Japs and asked to be shot in the head, but the Japs would laughingly shoot or bayonet them in the stomach. When the men cried out for another bullet to put them out of their misery the Japs continued to make merry and left the men to suffer, twelve men being killed in this manner. Captain Sato, Commander of the Jap garrison at the camp, walked over to C.C. Smith and split his head open with his saber. The Japs started shooting everything in sight, poked guns into the foxholes and fired them, threw hand grenades, while throughout Sato was laughing and shouting urging the men to greater effort.[91]

---

91 *Ibid.,* 4–5.

This is the definition of a war crime. Planned at the top and in this case, enthusiastically carried out by all at that camp. The Japanese seemed to be so proud of themselves they had a loud celebration.[92] Men remained in this prison until they were liberated in April. During those months following this crime, prisoners were still beaten indiscriminately, to the great joy of the guards.[93] The people of the Philippines suffered as well and on a far larger scale.

The Zamboanga Peninsula is part of the island of Mindanao, connected to the main part of the island by the Panguil Isthmus. Its rugged geography, dense forest, and formidable mountains made it far from ideal for military operations. Mobility and speed seemed impossible. For the Japanese, it was perfect. They could make the 41st Infantry Division pay for every inch of ground, fighting from positions both natural and manmade. Why enter this fight? Again, for the rationale behind this operation, one looks to the Eighth Army report on the campaign:

> In addition to the specific importance to the PHILIPPINE Liberation Campaign pointed out in the introduction to this report, the ZAMBOANGA-SULU region possesses a broad, general significance. The peninsula and its pendent islands lie at the intersection of two important sea-lanes; the north-south route from the NETHERLANDS EAST INDIES to CHINA and JAPAN and the east-west route from SAMOA and GUAM to the seaports of the PHILIPPINES and SINGAPORE. In addition, the peninsula and the archipelago dominate three vital waterways: BASILAN STRAIT between ZAMBOANGA and BASILAN ISLAND; SIBUTU PASSAGE at the center of the SULU ARCHIPELAGO; and ALICE CHANNEL in

---

92   *Ibid.,* 6.
93   *Ibid.,* 22.

the vicinity of TAWI TAWI. Here also are to be found the first, large and safe harbors on the southeast approach to the PHILIPPINES.

From this it can be seen that control of the ZAMBOANGA SULU region would deny all waters between BORNEO and the PHILIP-PINE ISLANDS to the Japanese, and afford air and naval bases for the coming assault on MIN-DANAO proper. Therefore, the seizure of these strategic areas was the logical prologue to the BORNEO landings and the ultimate clearance of the Southern Philippines.[94]

The above narrative is, in this historian's opinion, the result of loyalty from the Eighth Army commander, General Robert Eichelberger, to his superior, General Douglas MacArthur, and to the men of Eighth Army who fought on Zamboanga. It is not fortified by military reality. The US already controlled the air and sealanes in question with its aircraft carriers, submarines, and bases throughout the Philippines. Given Palawan's location, which the US controlled the day it landed, Zamboanga made no sense. If a Japanese ship, to reach the home islands, were to sail between Palawan and Zamboanga, and then proceed north through the remainder of the Philippines Archipelago, then it made military sense. A ship captain or military strategist did not exist who would undertake such an insane trip. This operation was to capture Japanese held territory, plain and simple. That alone is a valid reason, but subterfuge replaced the obvious.

The 41st Infantry Division's 162nd and 163rd RCTs were the primary force for Zamboanga. Initial estimates had 4,500 Japanese troops in the Peninsula, but two weeks before the invasion, that number had nearly doubled to 8,900.[95] This knowledge came

---

94 Eighth Army, *Report of the Commanding General Eighth Army on the Palawan and Zamboanga Operation*, 37.

95 *Ibid.,* 43.

from a well-organized guerrilla network. This network also told the Americans that their intended landing near San Mateo, a few miles north of the peninsula's main city, Zamboanga City, would be unopposed and that the Japanese had moved a few miles inland to high ground, which provided a perfect view of the vital airfield and the entire beach area.[96] Before the main landings at San Mateo, several companies of the 24th Infantry Division landed on the Peninsula's northern coast near Diplog. A needed airfield was there and it was under guerrilla control. Once the 24th arrived, so did a squadron of fighter-bombers and they stood ready to support the invasion. This quick precursor to the main attack was made all the more vital by the failure to have the airfields on Palawan ready.[97] On March 10, the 162nd and 163rd landed.

As with Palawan, the initial landings were relatively easy. As the two regiments moved inland, they discovered:

> The Japanese held a strong defensive position blocking the Santa-Maria-Pasananca Road at the base of mountains rising abruptly to 2000 feet within five miles of the coast. Their lines were anchored by artillery in strongly built earth and log bunkers, and in caves, and notably by vicious little 20mm dual purpose AckAck cannon. The black earth hills were abrupt and slippery and difficult even afoot. No longer did we have the abundant cover and low visibility of the New Guinea jungles. At long range, snipers could dominate the gaps and the ridge crests. The Regiment was committed to open fighting in wide aisled coconut plantations, and among scattered cultivated fields.[98]

96   Smith, 592.
97   *Ibid.,* 591.
98   163rd Infantry Regiment, *Historical Reports: V-4 Operation: Zamboanga*

It was not easy, but the Japanese defenses were quickly overcome. The land near the beaches was sturdy enough to support tanks and along with heavy artillery support and precision air strikes (by Marine Corps fighter-bombers), the initial enemy defenses were overcome. As the 162nd and 163rd advanced on March 12, they encountered "Blowout Hill," a position that truly earned its nickname.

The Japanese had a plentiful supply of naval shells, aerial bombs, and landmines and hoped to use them to delay, if not annihilate, significant parts of the US force. "Blowout Hill" was packed with this type of ordnance. The 163rd, on its way to Pasananca, occupied the hill. Just as suddenly as the hill was occupied, the Japanese "exploded an entire hill under the feet of our advance."[99] Thankfully, the Japanese had detonated too soon and casualties were lighter than they could have been: five dead and 40 wounded.[100] Japanese mines and booby traps became a major concern, but valuing speed more than caution (engineers could not keep up), the advance continued. On March 13, what was believed to be a dump for torpedoes exploded, causing another 65 US casualties.[101] Between March 14 and 17, progress was slow and advances meager at best. The terrain was rougher, making the employment of tanks impossible and a shortage of artillery ammunition somewhat, although not decisively, limited support there.[102] Nevertheless by March 24, when tank support was once again available, the Japanese resistance broke and mopping up operations, a task the Eighth Army repeatedly performed, began.

For the most part, mopping up involved chasing scattered Japanese elements around Zamboanga and once locating them, dig-

---

(Headquarters: 163rd Infantry Regiment, 41st Infantry Division, 1945), 1.

99   *Ibid.*

100   *Ibid.*

101   Eighth Army, *Report of the Commanding General Eighth Army on the Palawan and Zamboanga Operation*, 53.

102   *Ibid.*, 48.

ging them out of whatever position they occupied. A few more protracted fights did happen. The small island of Jolu is right next to the Zamboanga Peninsula. It was subjected to four days of artillery and airstrikes. A battalion of the 41st Infantry Division attacked on April 20 and encountered vicious enemy fire, resulting in three killed and 29 wounded. Artillery fire resumed and on April 22, 37 Marine aircraft, several of which were armed with rockets, hit the target area. Another advance secured the island with no further casualties to US forces. A total of 230 enemy dead were identified, although many more were believed sealed in the island's various caves. The Zamboanga campaign was over.[103]

In the last paragraph of the official campaign narrative, the Eighth Army stated: "These successful operations in the far south helped to isolate the Japanese remaining on Mindanao and placed our forces in control of potential air and naval bases which could now be used to neutralize enemy air opposition and attempts at ground reinforcement from the NETHERLANDS EAST INDIES."[104] This final explanation is as nonsensical as the original rationale for the campaign. The Japanese forces remaining on Mindanao were outflanked and isolated the moment US forces landed on Leyte.

No bases of any significance were operating from Zamboanga by the end of the war. No reinforcements from the Netherlands East Indies, the few that may have been sent from there, were ever intercepted by US forces on Zamboanga. The Japanese garrison, what was found of it, was destroyed (5,000 dead, 1,100 prisoners).[105] The rest of the enemy force, nearly 1,500 men, hid in the hills until war's end. US losses were 220 killed and 665 wounded.[106]

---

103 Ibid., 58–60.

104 *Ibid.*, 60.

105 Smith, 597.

106 *Ibid.*

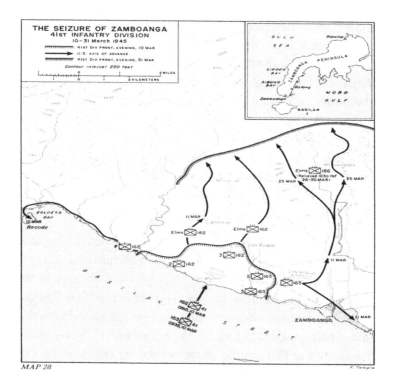

MAP 28

There was little to no doubt in the eyes of either the Japanese or Americans that the US would prevail in this battle. Several factors, some positive, others negative, became obvious by the conclusion of the campaign. Tanks, so often a positive contributor in the vicious fighting in the Pacific, were still a formidable weapon. However, the manner in which they were employed left a bit to be desired. Early in the campaign, US tanks played a significant role. The terrain favored their employment, but as the battle moved inland, vehicle movement was confined to the roads. The Japanese placed old naval depth charges on the roads, funneling US armor into heavy anti-tank fire.[107] Machine gun fire devastated accompanying infantry, many of whom, at tank commander insistence, rode on the tanks themselves, elevated

---

107 Eighth Army, *Report of the Commanding General Eighth Army on the Palawan and Zamboanga Operation*, 73.

and exposed. This was an ineffective way to employ both infantry and armor. It was noted that "had the tanks relied on infantry rifle fire for close-in protection and moved forward aggressively, they could have destroyed the enemy guns, thus insuring a rapid advance .... During the remainder of the fighting in this hill country, the infantry adhered to its organic weapons, artillery and air strikes to neutralize enemy resistance."[108] This clearly had to be addressed before any future operations. The 41st Infantry Division was earmarked for the invasion of Japan and spent the rest of the war refitting and training for an operation that thankfully did not take place.

Guerrilla units once again played a role in a Southern Philippines operation. At the end of fighting, a clearer picture of their capabilities and how they should be employed was obvious to the Eighth Army. The official campaign report noted "that they are adept at reconnaissance, patrolling, and ambushes and are valuable at preparing road blocks in the hinterland. However, it is a mistake to use them in the attack as they are critically short of equipment and have little understanding of the tactical principles involved in offensive combat."[109] Guerrilla reports on enemy strength also left something to be desired but were helpful in detailing "Japanese activities, combat effectiveness, and defensive installations."[110] Filipino guerrillas played a role in these operations, but it had to be a non-combat role.

In an earlier chapter, the debilitating effect of prolonged combat on several of the Sixth Army's divisions on Luzon was briefly explored. For the Sixth, 25th, and 32nd Infantry Divisions, the non-battle casualties exceeded those lost in combat. The Eighth Army divisions were not fighting as long and did not face as numerous an enemy. At Palawan and Zamboanga, casualties never reached a level where medical services were overwhelmed. Neu-

---

108 *Ibid.*, 74.

109 *Ibid.*, 75.

110 *Ibid.*, 94.

ropsychiatric cases, what we today would call PTSD, were rare on Palawan, as there was no sustained combat. That changed on Zamboanga. The fighting was much heavier and lasted several weeks. As the pace of combat picked up, so did the number of neurological cases. One could only imagine the impact on a soldier's mindset had they been on Blowout Hill when it exploded. Treatment was vital and thanks to a proactive medical officer, mild cases of mental exhaustion were given several days of rest, while more serious cases went to a special section of the division hospital and received help from actual psychiatrists. Shortages of men did not afflict the Eighth Army as it did the Sixth, and men clearly unable to return to combat were not sent there. There is little indication in the official records of the over 20 divisions I have thoroughly examined for three books and several articles on the Southwest Pacific Area (SWPA) that measures taken by the 41st Infantry Division were taken elsewhere. This was not due to a lack of concern, but to the sad fact that a true understanding of PTSD did not yet exist. This phase of the operation was over, although the Eighth Army returned to Mindanao soon thereafter. When looking back on Zamboanga, the 41st Infantry Division, veteran unit that it was, noted:

> When the veterans of the 163rd Infantry debate as to which of their three great Japanese battles was the hardest, they come to this conclusion. Sanananda was horrible because of its swamps and malaria. Biak was deadly because of the jagged jungled coral ridges and its invisible death. But the Zamboanga battle will best be remembered for the greatest concentration of artillery that the Regiment has ever fought its way through.[111]

---

111 163rd Infantry Regiment, *Historical Reports: V-4 Operation: Zamboanga*, 3.

V

Gruesome evidence of the hopeless situation into which the enemy had been forced after his evacuation of Ilolio was furnished by the account given by two Filipino women, who with four Jap babies were the only survivors of the mass suicide and murder of 62 Japanese civilians in the area south of Jimanban. A group of Jap soldiers, their flight apparently slowed by the civilians whom they had forced or persuaded to evacuate with them from the city, were overtaken by our troops. Driven to a final stand, they stabbed and bayonetted the women and children prior to their own destruction by our fire.

—40th Infantry Division[112]

As the Eighth Army cleared Palawan and the Zamboanga Peninsula, they looked ahead to the central Visayan islands of Panay, Negros, and Cebu. Of the three, Panay was the easiest operation, in many ways mirroring the seamless invasion of Palawan. Negros and Cebu were far more difficult. Each of these operations only required a single division. The 40th Infantry Division handled both Panay and Negros, the Americal Division Cebu. The Eighth Army played a very minor role in these campaigns. Thus far, General Eichelberger had been able to stay in the background, his presence unnecessary. That did not change until the invasion of Mindanao.

To understand why these operations were deemed necessary, the Eighth Army's report noted:

---

112 40th Infantry Division, *The Years of World War II*, 124 (Washington, DC: Army & Navy Publishing, 1947).

From a purely strategic viewpoint, the southern VISAYAS are less significant than their northern neighbors; but they could not be dismissed lightly from the overall plan of the war in the PACIFIC. Their occupation was important to the Allied strategy for the following reasons:

(1) They control the vital inland water passages connecting the VISAYAN, MINDANAO, and SULU SEAS

(2) They provide more than a score of well-situated airfields

(3) They are the principal food-producing area of the PHILIPPINES

(4) CEBU CITY is the second most important harbor and industrial center in the PHILIPPINES

The Eighth Army's amphibious strikes in the southern VISAYAS, therefore, were designed to consolidate our hold on the entire archipelago by giving us access to the vital waterways, strategic airfields, and natural resources of the rich heartland of the Philippines.[113]

As with the rationales for Palawan and Zamboanga, this is essentially obfuscation and hyperbole. The islands controlled the inner Filipino waterways, but the US already dominated those seas and the Japanese did not have the air or naval strength to contest it. There were already plenty of airfields. The principal food-producing region of the Philippines was Luzon's central plain and Cagayan Valley, not the Visayans. Cebu City was the Philippines second most important harbor and industrial center, but no bas-

---

113 Eighth Army, *Report of the Commanding General Eighth Army on the Panay-Negros and Cebu Operations, Victor I and II* (Headquarters: Eighth Army, 1945), 12.

es were established on that island before war's end, so its value was meaningless. As with other operations, the retaking of land was the sole purpose.

Panay, the westernmost of the Visayans, had the smallest garrison of the three. Only 2,750 Japanese personnel occupied the island, 1,500 of them combat troops. Included in the 2,750 were 400 Japanese civilians. Ilolio, home to a substantial harbor and several excellent airfields, was the obvious target for US forces. This was also obvious to Lt. Colonel Ryoichi Totsuka, the Japanese commander. The landings occurred on March 18, 1945, the first unit ashore was the 40th 185th RCT. Rather than fight and be annihilated, the Japanese retreated to the hills and by March 25, other than a few limited skirmishes, the battle was over. The 185th moved to Negros and a single battalion assumed control of the island, along with an effective, substantial guerrilla force. Totsuka surrendered at the end of the war with 1,560 men. US losses were 20 killed and 50 wounded.[114]

Panay was easy and a big part of that credit belongs to the island's guerrilla force. Its leader was a thirty-year-old Filipino, Colonel Macario Peralta.[115] His force dwarfed the Japanese on the island. Totsuka had 2,750 personnel, not all of them combat troops. Peralta had 22,500 officers and men, although only half of them were armed.[116] They harassed the Japanese continuously, avoiding set battles, but conducting effective raids and ambushes. Reprisals by the Japanese against Panay's civilian population were harsh and that created the problem of just how active the guerrillas should be. They remained very active. Peralta's guerrillas controlled most of the island, pinpointed Japan's major positions, and operated several airfields on the northern part of the island.[117] From

---

114 Smith, 601–02.

115 *The Guerilla Resistance Movement In The Philippines*, 48.

116 Eighth Army, *Report of the Commanding General Eighth Army on the Panay-Negros and Cebu Operations, Victor I and II*, 18.

117 40th Infantry Division, *The Years of World War II*, 121.

those airfields, artillery spotter planes, arriving a few days before the invasion, were able to observe the entire landing area. When the landings began, the men of the 185th RCT were greeted by Peralta's men. Negros was a far tougher fight.

Panay was an easy military campaign for the Eighth Army. For the natives of the island, it was a hard four years. The Japanese garrison rampaged continuously on Panay. One such rampage happened during an approximate two-week period in September 1943. In the towns of Ajuy and Sara, the Japanese "indiscriminately tortured and murdered men, women, and children in an attempt to learn of and suppress guerilla activities, or to terrorize the civilians."[118] Between 500 and 600 civilians were murdered by crucifixion, children were hung upside down from trees and their skulls bashed in against the bodies of their murdered mothers, and countless women were repeatedly raped.[119] A surviving witness recounted:

> On September 18, 1943 while my family and I were attempting to evacuate from our home, we were apprehended by Captain Fuji and his men who had just penetrated the barrio. Immediately after our arrest we were taken by the Japanese to the house of Cesario Demonteverde. My son, Basilio Pasadas, 16 years old, and I were tied to a banana tree near this house. The rest of my family, along with 42 other people who had been made prisoners previously, were taken inside the house. After a few minutes, I heard screams of terror and pain coming from the house. Then I saw the Japanese soldiers leave the house and set fire to it. They untied us and I went to the ruins

---

118 Theater Judge Advocate, *Murder, Torture, and Rape in the Towns of Ajuy and Sara, Iloilo Province, P.I., between 13 September 1943 and 29 September 1943* (General Headquarters: United States Army Forces, Pacific, Office Of The Theater Judge Advocate, War Crimes Branch, 1945), 1.

119 *Ibid.*

of the house where I saw the charred bodies of the victims.[120]

The woman who witnessed this atrocity later saw her son and 11 others be murdered as they moved to another town. Upon reaching that town, approximately 50 civilians were murdered: the old men and women beheaded and the children clubbed to death.[121] This murderous spree continued in 1944, although only few of the acts are documented.

During the first half of 1944, witnesses detailed the murder of 65 men, women, and children and the attempted murder of many more (beheadings, beatings, hangings).[122] On November 7, another group of Japanese soldiers, searching for guerillas and US forces that would not arrive for another six months, tortured several women and then murdered their entire family.[123] A witness to these murders also saw an old man beheaded and heard stories of 26 others suffering a similar fate (all relatives of supposed guerillas).[124] A Japanese soldier told this individual that he and his squad had embarked on an expedition in search of guerillas and having come up empty, indiscriminately murdered a family of four.[125] These are but some of the documented cases on Panay; there were more. In history, brutality seems to coexist with guerilla movements. That is not the case here. The Japanese history of brutality throughout Asia existed regardless of the presence of guerillas.

---

120 *Ibid.,* 4.

121 *Ibid.,* 5.

122 Theater Judge Advocate, *Murder of Filipino Civilians at Miagao, Ilolio Province, Panay, P.I.* (General Headquarters: United States Army Forces, Pacific, Office Of The Theater Judge Advocate, War Crimes Branch, 1945), 1–8.

123 Theater Judge Advocate, *Murder of Members of the Jaguren Family and Others on 7 November 1944* (General Headquarters: United States Army Forces, Pacific, Office Of The Theater Judge Advocate, War Crimes Branch. 1945), 1–6.

124 *Ibid.,* 9.

125 *Ibid.,* 10.

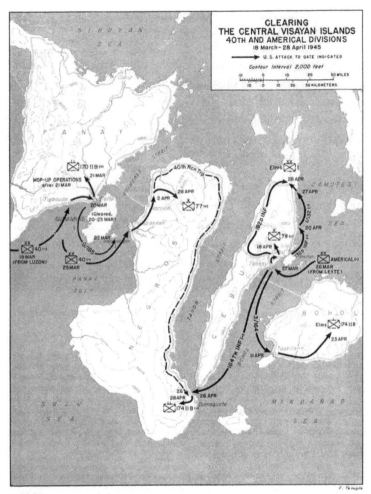

MAP 30

Negros became a fight on the island's rugged mountains between the 40th Infantry Division and a determined, resourceful Japanese garrison of approximately 13,500 men under the command of Lt. General Takeshi Kono.[126] Many of the enemy soldiers lacked basic infantry weapons, and commodities such as food were also in short supply. They had plentiful artillery and auto-

---

126 Smith, 605.

matic weapons, something US troops had to deal with as they dug the Japanese out of their positions. As had become the general trend in these operations, Kono did not intend to contest the landings or any of the few key points on the island.[127] Northern Negros' mountains were also covered with rainforest. Earlier, the flawed rationale for these operations was alluded to. In the same report that explained why Panay, Negros, and Cebu possessed tactical and strategic value, the Eighth Army stated: "The unbroken coastline contains few bays or inlets; no harbors suitable for large vessels exist."[128] This island could never be used as a staging area for future Filipino operations, let alone an invasion of Japan. There were numerous airstrips, some of which required major upgrades, but the US already had plenty of those. The Japanese had utilized Negros' vast sugar plantations for the production of alcohol-based fuel and the world's largest hardwood sawmill for building and construction materials.[129]

The Negros landings began on March 29, 1945. Given the outlook of the Japanese commander, it should come as no surprise that the initial beach landings were unopposed. To get inland, the Bago River Bridge had to be secured. It was 650 feet long and US engineers estimated that under the best of conditions it would take a month to replace.[130] Such a delay could be dangerous for a force confined to a beachhead. A daring platoon, a single platoon, seized the bridge. An Eighth Army observer detailed the entire action, a few hours before the main landings happened:

> At 0505 in the pre-dawn darkness of 29 March, four and one-half hours before the division landing was made at PULUPANDAN, Second

---

127 Ibid.

128 Eighth Army, *Report of the Commanding General Eighth Army on the Panay-Negros and Cebu Operations, Victor I and II*, 6.

129 40th Infantry Division, *The Years of World War II*, 126.

130 Eighth Army, *Report of the Commanding General Eighth Army on the Panay-Negros and Cebu Operations, Victor I and II*, 33.

Lieutenant Aaron A. Hanson and a reinforced platoon from Company F, 185th Infantry, left their ship in two landing craft (mechanized), one of them a rocket type, and one small landing craft (support). As they approached PULUPANDAN, they turned south and sailed 100 yards offshore for a mile and a half before landing at PATIK town.

During this overwater movement, they feared that the rumble of their boats' engines would be heard by enemy forces in the town, thereby betraying their arrival. The noise did arouse PATIK, but only friendly townsfolk met the party when it landed 100 yards south of the town.

They moved inland rapidly along the south side of the road leading due east to Highway No. 1. Before crossing the highway they were met by a sergeant of the guerrilla intelligence who told them that a party of nine Japanese with three ox-carts was moving along the PATIK road toward the vital BAGO RIVER bridge.

As they crossed Highway No. 1, they sighted the enemy group and, simultaneously, the Japanese saw Lieutenant Hanson's platoon. Dropping off a small force with a radio, the Lieutenant began a race with the enemy to the bridge. His party drove forward on the soft ground to the right of the road while the Japanese advanced on the hard-surfaced road itself. A quick estimate of the situation indicated to Lieutenant Hanson that the enemy's objective was to reach the bridge before his platoon but that gunfire at this point would warn the bridge guards.

At 0730 Lieutenant Hanson's platoon intercepted the enemy near the approach to the bridge and opened fire. The initial volley killed the oxen and four Japanese, the remainder taking cover. The bridge guards now entered the action, and the platoon was subjected to converging small arms and machine-gun fire from both the bridge and the Japanese detachment from PULUPAN-DAN. After establishing a base of fire with two light machine guns and a 60mm mortar to keep the enemy on the north bank pinned down, Lieutenant Hanson deployed his men for an enveloping attack to seize the bridge.

The platoon charged the bridge. Private First Class Vinthers, an assistant automatic rifleman, took the lead, killing the guard at the bridge entrance. About a quarter of the way across, the platoon was pinned down by intense fire from the far side. Private First Class Vinthers again took the lead, killing one Japanese at a mine control point in the center of the bridge before he could push the plunger of the electrical detonator. Vinthers, who was awarded the Distinguished Service Cross posthumously for his bravery, was killed 20 yards beyond this point. One more Japanese was killed on the far side while the remainder dispersed.

At 0745, the bridge was overrun and reported secure at 0800. At this time, however, the platoon was again subjected to enemy fire from Japanese machine guns and mortars emplaced about 500 yards northeast of the bridge.

At 0830, the rear element with the radio reported that natives had warned them of the approach of 60 Japanese and nine oxcarts moving up from VALLADOLID. Hanson immediately prepared to meet this new threat. He placed one squad with one machine gun, one Browning automatic rifle, and one sub-machine gun at the northeast end of the bridge. The balance of the platoon with the mortar, bazooka, machine gun, three automatic rifles, and three Thompson sub-machine guns, were deployed on the southwest side of the bridge thereby covering the highway leading to the bridge. The Japanese appeared at 0850 and Hanson's group opened fire, taking them completely by surprise. They killed two and wounded an unknown number. The survivors escaped, taking their wounded and their weapons with them but leaving all the carts, two of which contained high explosives and wooden land mines. The other carts were filled with ammunition, clothing, rations and cooking equipment.

The platoon held the bridge until the main force, which landed at 0930, crossed enroute to BACOLOD.[131]

It was a remarkable achievement. The loss of that bridge could have been dangerous for the 40th Infantry Division, a forced crossing of a river with the enemy looking down on them, all the while building an actual bridge. A brave platoon made that unnecessary.

Three regimental combat teams, the 40th 160th and 185th and the attached 503d Parachute Infantry Regiment, did the fighting on Negros. After successfully seizing the Bago River Bridge, the 160th and 185th headed inland, and the 503rd joined the fight

---

131 *Ibid.,* 29–30.

on April 9. They met no real resistance. Baolod, the first major objective, was seized after a quick fight (most of the enemy garrison retreated north). Enemy units all headed for the refuge of the mountains and it became a contest to see if they could get there before US units, primarily the 185th RCT, could stop them. They could not advance as fast as the Japanese retreated. Nevertheless, within a week, most of Negros's western coast was in US hands.[132] Guerrillas controlled most of the southern part of the island.

Guerrillas played a role on Negros, as they did on other Filipino islands. For years, various factions had fought each other as much as the Japanese. By 1944, a coherent organization under the command of Lt. Colonel Salvador Abcede roamed the island. They informed the 40th that most of the Japanese garrison had moved north. They provided information on Japanese positions, acted as guides, and gave accounts of the full measure of Japanese atrocities on the island.[133] Were they effective militarily? Lt. Colonel Charles Etzler, commander of the 185th RCT's 3rd Battalion noted: "I don't want to give the impression that the Guerrillas were sufficiently strong in men, equipment, or supplies to fight a pitched battle with the Nips, but they did prevent the enemy from being able to exploit the resources of the whole island, and thereby dealt the Jap a hard blow where he was weakest, in the 'breadbasket.'"[134] Not decisive, but certainly helpful. Abcede's guerrillas continued to deal with the southern part of Negros and the 40th moved north, launching a major offensive on April 9.

The ease of the advance was about to change. The 40th now faced:

> rugged terrain where the Japanese had every
> defensive advantage. Kono's men had prepared
> cave and bunker positions, most of them mutual-

---

132 40th Infantry Division, *The Years of World War II*, 129.

133 *The Guerilla Resistance Movement In The Philippines*, 69.

134 Lt. Colonel Charles R. Etzler, *The Japanese Defense Of The Island of Negros (Occidental) P.I.* (Fort Leavenworth, KS: Command and General Staff College, 1947).

ly supporting and many connected by tunnels or trenches. The Japanese had dug tank traps along all roads and trails in the mountains, and had also laid minefields using aerial bombs. Kono's men had excellent observation, for most of the hills in their last-stand area were open, grass covered, and steep sided. During daylight, the Japanese were content to conduct a static defense, but they undertook harassing attacks almost every night .... The battle soon denigrated into mountain warfare of the roughest sort involving all the problems, frustrations, delays, failures, and successes that American troops were encountering in the mountains of Luzon. The 40th Division employed air and artillery support liberally, but in the end, as on Luzon, had to close with each individual position with flamethrowers and the rifle-carrying infantrymen.[135]

The first Japanese defensive line, centered on the town of San Juan, was taken on April 11. By the 14th, the high ground around the town was taken. Operating with three regiments abreast (the 503rd to the north, the 160th RCT to the south, and the 185th RCT in the center), the 40th for two days pounded enemy positions with continuous artillery fire, while air power launched mission after mission.[136] Heavy rains postponed the attack for a day, but on the 17th, the infantry attack commenced. Heavy resistance was immediately encountered. The Japanese positions were destroyed, but in slow, costly operations. Tanks were used whenever possible, but as the division entered higher ground, the terrain was no longer conducive to armored support. Further, the Japanese did all they could to limit US employment of their

---

135 Smith, 607.

136 40th Infantry Division, *Operations Report: 18 March–20 June 45, Victor I: Panay, Victor II: Negros* (Headquarters: 40th Infantry Division, 1945), 19.

tanks, recognizing how quickly they turned the tide of an engagement. A tank trap, located west of San Juan demonstrates how far the Japanese went to keep tanks away:

> The trap, dug to a depth of eighteen feet at a point where the road narrowed to a bare ten feet by sheer cliffs on either side, was covered by enemy fire. Self-propelled weapons could not be brought forward to support the infantry until the high ground beyond was secured to permit bulldozers to fill the trap. Repeated attacks were launched against the hostile positions. Each time the attackers were subjected to heavy mortar concentrations and artillery fire. After two days of bitter fire the area was finally cleared, bulldozers had repaired the road, and tanks rumbled forward.[137]

This tank trap was made by the Japanese. Others, like Dolan Hill, were formidable with or without any Japanese assistance.

Dolan Hill, so named after the first officer killed in the attempt to seize it, was a typical Japanese position. Steep and overgrown with vegetation, it was a treacherous advance, soldiers often grasping branches and grass in order to scale the hill.[138] Ground was gained during the day, and at night, the Japanese, with frequent harassing attacks and attempted infiltration, tried to take it back. Before the initial assault, heavy artillery and air attacks pounded Dolan Hill for two days. The infantry advance that followed seemed to go well as they managed to reach a point only a few hundred feet from the crest of the hill. The enemy still looked down on them and at night poured fire and everything else they had down on the US infantry. The volume of enemy fire and the lack of heavy weapons with which to respond, as the ground was

---

137 *Ibid.*

138 40th Infantry Division, *The Years of World War II*, 132.

too steep to bring it to their position, forced a temporary US withdrawal.[139]

The 40th ID's 160th RCT continued trying to reach the top of Dolan Hill:

> Several attempts to reach the crest met with the same determined resistance. Air and artillery blasted the enemy location, but their well-prepared positions withstood the pounding and results were negligible .... His defensive positions had been cleverly designed. Personnel caves on the reverse slope of the knoll were connected by a network of communications trenches to mutually supporting pillboxes well-hidden on the narrow ridge. High on the crest of the hill in rear of these positions, machine guns sighted to cover the forward positions were later found.[140]

If the Japanese defenses in of themselves were not enough, the 160th could not outflank the enemy because of the steep and rocky terrain. Supplies and heavy weapons were in short supply since the only way to get them up the hill was by carrying them, and it rained constantly. Growing frustration with such a stalemate led to four full days of air attacks and all the division's artillery engulfing the hill. On Day 5, advancing behind a creeping artillery barrage, the infantry reached the crest of the hill. They found: "once dense vegetation had been completely cleared, not a leaf remained on the bare tree stumps, 41 enemy pillboxes were found blasted to bits, over 200 enemy dead were discovered and our troops moved to the crest unopposed."[141] As the advance continued, both the 160th and 185th RCTs methodically dug and blasted the Japanese out of their holes, caves,

---

139 *Ibid.,* 132–34.

140 *Ibid.,* 134.

141 *Ibid.,* 133.

and pillboxes. The 503rd RCT, an airborne unit, was having a far harder time.

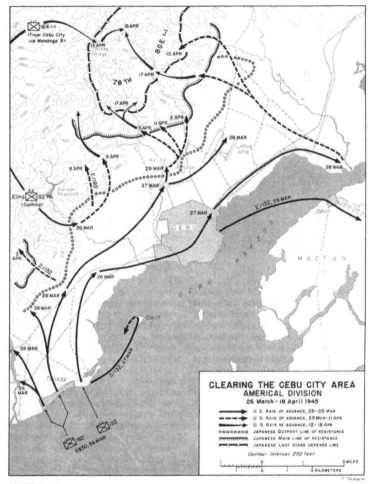

MAP 31

The 160th and 185th RCTs were standard infantry regiments. They had worked with tanks, had trained at isolating and destroying Japanese positions, and understood the value of their division's abundant, organic artillery. The 503rd was far below the strength of a standard infantry regiment. For the three months they spent on Negros, the regiment was usually below half strength.[142] The 503rd made the following observations about their time on Negros:

1. Phase I had ended. Nothing like it had we seen before or would see during the remainder of the war. It was a slugging infantry war. We were a lightly armed airborne unit and had to learn to fight with heavy support, i.e., tanks, self-propelled guns, heavy mortars and heavier artillery. We had to learn at the expense of good men's lives.

2. We are learning to use our artillery and heavy mortar support more and more. Many lives were saved by this properly used support. Most, if not all of the Jap prepared defensive positions encountered on Negros were positions that denied flanking movements, so frontal attacks had to be made. The only sane method of combatting such positions was to blast them out with artillery and mortars.

3. ... we all could see the mountains to the East, and we knew that the Japanese had been slowly falling back towards them (about 6 miles in 21 days). We weren't overjoyed either as the ground to our front got higher and higher and we were assaulting ridge after ridge .... A movie concerning Negros could very well have been called "The Jap Always Have The High Ground."[143]

Note, "learning" to use their heavy support. Dismayed by the constant high ground before them. Frustrated with their lack of ground troops. An airborne unit is born with the idea of speed and mobility. They train for speed and mobility. This was the absolute worst type of fight for them. While ultimately successful, the airborne was in far worse shape than their infantry brothers by the end of the campaign.

---

142 John Reynolds, *Partial History Of The 503d Negros Mission*, http://corre gidor.org/503_reynolds/1.htm.

143 *Ibid.*

By the middle of May, the Japanese had scattered into the hills. Patrolling continued and several smaller battles occurred, but the outcome was never in doubt. The Japanese lost 7,525 men in the Negros operation (4,000 to US fire, the remainder to starvation and disease), while US losses were also heavy, 381 dead and 1,061 wounded.[144] Where were the remaining men of the enemy garrison? Hiding in Negros' thick northern mountains. 6,150 Japanese soldiers surrendered at war's end.[145] The Eighth Army saw this in all its operations.

The last of the Visayan Islands is Cebu. Panay and Negros had little value as a potential staging area for an invasion of Japan. Cebu did have practical military value. Cebu City is the Philippines' second largest city and its port and harbor facilities were extensive; although, as with the other islands invaded by the Eighth Army, Cebu was never developed to the point it could be used to support an invasion of Japan. The American Division (a standard infantry division, just not numbered) was tasked with conducting the Cebu operation. Before invading Cebu, the American participated in the mopping-up operations on Leyte. It began the invasion of Cebu with only two of its three infantry regiments. Initially, the American Division's 164th RCT remained on Leyte, completing its role of mopping up and garrisoning already secure areas. The division had lost several thousand of its number to action and exhaustion on Leyte, but as of the time of staging for Cebu, it had received no replacements. Once ashore, the Americal was the approximate equal of their enemy in number, never a promising scenario. The Japanese garrison of 14,500 men was centered on the ground above Cebu City (12,500) and the northern extreme of the island (2,000). Few of this number under the overall command of General Sosaku Suzuki, with General Takeo Manjome commanding the forces around Cebu City and General Tadasu Kataoka in the north, were actual combat troops, but

---

144 Eighth Army, *Report of the Commanding General Eighth Army on the Panay-Negros and Cebu Operations, Victor I and II*, 44.

145 Smith, 607.

that never really seemed to matter once the fighting began. All members of Japanese garrisons fought fanatically to the end. To offset his numerical deficiencies, General William Arnold, the Americal Division's commander, counted on the support of Cebu's large guerrilla force of 8,500 men under the command of Lt. Colonel James Cushing.[146]

Part of the responsibility the Americal Division placed with Cebu's guerrillas was in ascertaining Japanese numbers or any possible surprises the enemy may have created. They gave incorrect numbers and failed to inform the Eighth Army of the positions that the Japanese prepared or of a vast minefield hidden on the approaches to and on the landing beaches themselves.[147] From the beach to Cebu City, the main objective of the operation, obstacles, pillboxes, and a multitude of other Japanese positions could theoretically impede any advance by the Americal Division. Fortunately, no such resistance occurred. The landings began early on the morning of March 26. Immediately, 10 of the first 15 landing craft were knocked out by the mines.[148] The waters off the beach and the beach itself were quickly congested. It is standard military doctrine to cover an obstacle such as a minefield with direct observation and fire. The Japanese did not follow standard military doctrine. Following the same pattern as that employed on islands such as Panay and Negros, the Japanese had moved most of their forces into the hills above Cebu City, thus losing the opportunity to devastate the US landings when most vulnerable. Fortune favored the United States at this point in the war.

The Japanese created a formidable defensive system on Cebu. That came as no surprise, as the Japanese always created a formidable defensive system. However, on Cebu, there wasn't a singular line of defense, but one in depth. Manjome:

---

146 *Ibid.*, 608–10.

147 Robert C. Muehrcke, *Orchids In The Mud: Personal Accounts By Veterans Of The 132nd Infantry Regiment* (Chicago: J.S. Printing, 1985), 354.

148 Smith, 610.

designed his defenses as to control-not-hold-the coastal plains around Cebu City and for this purpose set up defenses in depth north and northwest of the city. A forward line, constituting an outpost line of resistance, stretched across the first rising ground behind the city, hills two and a half to four miles inland. A stronger and shorter second line, the main line of resistance, lay about a mile farther inland and generally 350 feet higher into the hills. Back of this MLR were Manjome's last-stand defenses, centering in rough, broken hills five miles or so north of the city.

... the inner defense lines were a system of mutually supporting machine gun positions in caves, pillboxes, and bunkers. Many of these positions had been completed for months and had acquired natural camouflage. Manjome's troops had an ample supply of machine guns and machine cannon and, like the Japanese on Negros, employed remounted aircraft and antiaircraft weapons.[149]

The above would be encountered after the initial landings and objectives were secure. The American's 132nd and 182nd Infantry Regiments were able to organize themselves after the chaos of the minefields. They quickly secured the docks and most of Cebu City by the 27th, although the Japanese destroyed much of the city before withdrawing. The heights dominated the city and to actually use the harbor (which again did not happen before the end of the war), the Japanese and their guns had to be silenced.

Along with the port, the most valuable position on Cebu was Lahug Airfield. As with the port and Cebu City itself, the airfield

---

149 *Ibid.*

was quickly seized. Also, as with the port and city, the Japanese occupied the heights above the airfield. To be able to operate safely from Lahug, several hills had to be taken. Hill 30 was the first step. Initially, guerrilla reports indicated they controlled the hill. When the 182nd arrived, they found it to be "crawling with Japanese."[150] Several assaults were repulsed. Part of the problem was the Americal Division was understrength; its 164th RCT did not arrive until April 9. Firepower replaced the lack of infantry. Tanks and self-propelled howitzers arrived and by the end of the day (March 28), the regiment had seized the hill, destroying 30 Japanese pillboxes in the process.[151] Go Chan Hill was next. Due to the thick terrain and steep heights, attacks were generally frontal and the Japanese poured fire down upon them. Even with tank support, the infantry had trouble. They pulled back to allow artillery and airpower to soften up the position. By the end of the day (March 29), a company of infantry reached the hilltop, only to have the Japanese blow up the hill (as they had done at Blow-out Hill on Negros) beneath them. Heavy casualties resulted. Go Chan Hill was finally secured on March 30, with the work done by a battalion of the 182nd, supported by two M-7 self-propelled howitzers.[152] Lahug Airfield was now safe for operations.

Cebu would have been easier if the Americal Division had entered the operation at full strength. As previously noted, the division's third regiment was scheduled to arrive on April 9. It would have made sense to wait for its arrival, but patience had never been a military value under MacArthur's command. Until April 9, there were not enough men to probe the full extent of Japanese positions, to flank those that were found, or to exploit any local success. Frontal attacks against "unknown" enemy positions on high ground were the only remedy and frustration mounted. General Arnold, in a report to General Eichelberger, noted:

---

150 Muehrcke, *Orchids In The Mud,* 362.

151 Cronin, 283.

152 Muehrcke, 362.

Situation has developed to the point that approximately two-thirds of the Japanese positions in the vicinity of CEBU CITY have been contacted. The Japanese left flank has not been determined. Positions now facing us are elaborately prepared for defense and include numerous tunnels, with interconnecting tunnels leading into heavily-constructed pillboxes. These positions are in every case on hills and are in depth. All avenues of approach are mined and barbed wire has been encountered. Many pillboxes are so strongly constructed that they withstand direct hits from 105s. The whole Japanese position is estimated to cover a distance of 20,000 yards around CEBU CITY area and is manned by approximately 7,500 troops. There is no indication that the enemy is short of ammunition, and he is well-equipped with light and heavy machine guns. Reconnaissance in force up Highway 1 northeast of CEBU CITY develops numerous Japanese in position armed with small arms, machine guns, heavy mortars, 75mm artillery, and possibly a heavier gun. The whole area is extensively mined. Enemy estimated in this area 1,000 to 1,500. Information believed to be reliable. Now have four battalions seriously engaged, and additional one is covering right flank. The remaining battalion will be required to determine and attack the left of the Japanese position. It is my considered opinion that operations will be slow and tedious and that expenditures of artillery ammunition will be high. Casualties are increasing and will continue to do so. LAHUG FIELD is intermittently harassed by 90mm and 20mm fire. This harassment will probably continue until we can drive well back into the mountains.[153]

The main Japanese position that General Arnold had to deal with was Babag Ridge, the anchor of which was Babag Mountain itself. It was approximately 1,900 feet high, typically steep and overgrown with jungle, and possessed an "exceptional view of the harbor, Cebu City, and the surrounding area."[154] The first attacks began on April 1, and it was three long weeks before the fight ended.

Attacks seemed to gain ground, only to be stopped by heavy Japanese fire. Many of the enemy pillboxes were made of coral, and even direct hits from tanks, self-propelled howitzers, and standard artillery did little damage.[155] The 132nd Infantry Regiment described the battle:

> Air bombardment and intense artillery fire preceded every American attack. The job was slow, dangerous and extremely costly. For the battle weary 132nd Infantry, it was the most difficult and most expensive fighting they had ever encountered. The cost in lives was high.
>
> When the American artillery, naval guns and intense air bombardment failed to reduce the Japanese stronghold, a difficult job fell to the infantry and combat engineers. To blast the Japanese out of their caves and their entrenched hill positions the infantry used their special skills. This was supported by flame throwers, bazookas, Bangalore torpedoes and satchel charges

---

153 Eighth Army, *Report of the Commanding General Eighth Army on the Panay-Negros and Cebu Operations, Victor I and II,* 66–67.

154 Muehrcke, 363.

155 *Ibid.*

of explosives but most of all Sherman tanks and
M-7's.[156]

What would one of these battles look like? A Japanese pillbox
would be spotted on the slope of Babag Mountain at an elevation
of approximately 100 feet. Heavy fire from that pillbox and several others higher up would wreak havoc on any and all advances. A platoon of infantry from the 1st Battalion, 182nd Infantry
Regiment would attack the pillbox at 1100 hours. It would be an
experienced platoon, particularly in dealing with static Japanese
positions. They would be a platoon of 30 men. Within that 30
would be three squads of 10, nine, and nine infantrymen. The two
nine man squads would have six riflemen, a Browning Automatic Rifle (BAR) operator, and a two man 30-caliber machine gun
team. Two of the six riflemen would also carry satchel charges.
The 10-man squad would be an assault team with two bazookas
(four men), a flamethrower (two men), and a Bangalore torpedo
team. The Platoon Leader and Platoon Sgt. would round out the
platoon. Two Sherman tanks would lead the advance, hoping to
draw enemy fire and allowing the assault team to get into position. The platoon would remain five hundred yards short of the
Japanese pillbox so artillery fire could hopefully neutralize it and
an air attack against the enemy positions further up the hill could
deprive it of support. The planes would appear at 1000 hours and
for a few ferocious minutes light up the mountain. At 1015 hours,
the division artillery (105mm and 155mm guns) would prep the
pillbox and surrounding area. At 1030 hours, the artillery would
shift its fire up the hill and the platoon would move out, the tanks
leading the way. Despite the air and artillery bombardments, as
the platoon advances to within approximately 100 yards of the
targeted pillbox, Japanese fire would erupt. One squad would
quickly lose two men, one killed, the other wounded. The tanks
would continue to advance, the infantry now using the armored
monsters as shields. The artillery would be doing an excellent job

---

156 *Ibid.*, 363–64.

of keeping the Japanese pillboxes on higher ground occupied and the tanks would be impervious to enemy machine guns and mortars. The two squads would deploy to either flank of the pillbox, their machine guns keeping up a steady stream of fire. This would allow the assault team's flame-thrower section to circle the position and burn it out. A satchel charge would then be thrown in. The tanks would continue to move forward. This pillbox would be the primary objective, but several others would be in close proximity. One would be engulfed in jungle and the tanks, fearful of losing a tread on unknown ground, and could go no further. The Bangalore torpedo section would move in and blow a wide space in the jungle, although two more men would be killed in the process. The ground would be strewn with holes, each large enough to immobilize the tanks. They would continue to fire on the pillboxes, as would the machine guns of the infantry squads. Several more pillboxes would be eliminated by bazookas, the flame-thrower, and the tanks. One would even be destroyed by an incredibly brave man who rushed in, climbed atop the pillbox, and dropped a hand grenade through a vision slit. All told, seven Japanese pillboxes would be destroyed and perhaps 50 enemy soldiers would be killed in addition to an unknown number buried in debris. The platoon would lose eight men, three killed, and five wounded. One hundred yards of ground would be gained. Much more would remain.

While hypothetical, the above was typical of the fights on Babag Mountain. When the 164th arrived the American Division finally had the manpower needed to secure the entire ridge, which they did on April 21. No battle in the Southwest Pacific Area was complete without an official statement from General MacArthur. True to form, on April 21, he stated:

> On Cebu our troops, in a wide enveloping movement which caught the enemy unawares, attacked his positions from the west flank and rear and completely defeated him. His losses

were very heavy, 5,000 dead being left in the field with remnants scattered into the hills to be hunted down by our guerrilla forces .... This virtually concluded the VISAYAN Campaign ... it sweeps clear the center of the PHILIPPINES and leaves the only remaining enemy organized resistance in upper LUZON on the north and MINDANAO on the south.[157]

Of course it was not the end of the Visayan campaign. "Mopping up" continued on Negros and Cebu until June, but General MacArthur never acknowledged such a phrase. His interest in Cebu disappeared once Cebu City was secure. Nor did he acknowledge the slow, costly fight the American Division encountered on the island, most of it without all their organic strength. General Eichelberger acknowledged this reality. While quick, he noted: "Considering the forces involved and their relative strengths the Babag Mountain position including Hills 25, 26, and 27 were the toughest to reduce ever."[158] The campaign officially ended on June 20. Japanese losses were 10,224 killed and 232 prisoners; US losses were 449 killed, 1,969 wounded, nine missing, and the unbelievable total of 8,000 non-battle casualties.[159]

Eight thousand non-battle casualties sounds like an enormous number, and it is. That is over half the American Division's full strength. Most of those 8,000 came in the month of April during the heaviest fighting.[160] An epidemic of hepatitis and, to a smaller extent, dysentery ravaged the division's ranks. Many of these attacks that were of the frontal variety or limited in scope devel-

---

157 Eighth Army. *Report of the Commanding General Eighth Army on the Panay-Negros and Cebu Operations, Victor I and II,* 68.

158 Muehrcke, 364–65.

159 Smith, 617.

160 Eighth Army, *Report of the Commanding General Eighth Army on the Panay-Negros and Cebu Operations, Victor I and II,* 96.

oped out of necessity, as men were sick. This is important to consider because both the Japanese and the division itself were very critical of the America's performance in this battle. The Japanese had no knowledge of the epidemic, while the Americal Division reports either ignore it or act as if it were just an excuse.

Colonel Satushi Wada was the Chief of Staff of the Japanese 102rd Division, the principal combat formation on Cebu. After the war he offered the following appraisal of the Americal:

> the Americal Division had been inordinately slow in mounting envelopments ... the frontal attack in the center had been wasteful of time and lives and the Americal would have done better to execute an early, strong envelopment of the Japanese left via the Butuanoan Valley. He felt that the Mananga River envelopment, on the Japanese right, had started too late and had been too weak to achieve much significance.[161]

These observations were made to Robert Ross Smith, the Army's official historian of the entire Philippine campaign. Smith notes that Wada did not consider the Americal lacking all three of its regiments or its lack of knowledge of the exact extent of the Japanese line.[162] The effects of the non-battle casualties are also not considered. The Division's own history also does not consider the aforementioned factors.

The following are excerpts from a publication of the Americal Division titled "Lessons Learned in Combat–Cebu-V-2 Operations." After Action Reports are designed to be critical so mistakes are not repeated and a unit continues to tactically grow. Here there is plenty of criticism, but no acknowledgement of the division's limited strength and why the strength was so limited:

---

161 Smith, 616.

162 *Ibid.*

1. Often the lack of aggressiveness was evident. Entire platoons would consider themselves pinned down when receiving fire from only 3 to 4 riflemen. In some cases, platoon leaders would withdraw their platoons, or else formulate an entire new plan for attacking the objective and put it into effect without informing all individuals within the platoon or obtaining permission from the next higher commander.

2. In many cases too much reliance was placed on other than organic weapons. Artillery, tanks, air, etc. have a definite plan but the infantry cannot expect their objective to be smashed altogether by outside means

3. Some units showed unwillingness to advance as long as enemy fire was being received. Rather, these units stopped completely and engaged the enemy in long drawn out firefights, where a quick advance by fire and movement to the Jap positions would have succeeded and casualties among our own troops would have been lighter

4. There were many cases where the effect of artillery, mortar, and the base of fire was lost because the infantry did not follow it up immediately. During the interval between cease firing of support weapons and the infantry attack the enemy regained from the shock and was able to bring fire on the assaulting troops as soon as they jumped off.[163]

These criticisms would have far more credence if the division had been at full strength during the battle or if US heavy weapons had been able to more effectively reduce Japanese positions. When the sick began to ravage ranks even further, the type of aggressiveness noted above was extremely dangerous to the survival of

---

163 Americal Division, *Lessons Learned in Combat–Cebu-V-2 Operations* (Headquarters: Americal Division, 1945), 1–2.

even the smallest combat element. Given the circumstances, the Americal Division did an outstanding job on Cebu.

Cebu also has documented cases of Japanese atrocities against the native population. A family near the town of Cabatangan was viciously murdered by the Japanese. The father was beaten and taken away, never to be seen again. His wife was beaten and several soldiers attempted to rape her. The whole family received no food or water for three days.[164] In the weeks before the US landings on Cebu, a plane was shot down and its crew captured. A hole was dug, the two US airmen made to kneel, and they were beheaded. Five Filipino civilians in the vicinity, for the simple reason they were in the vicinity, suffered a similar fate.[165] Many of the perpetrators of these atrocities were never brought to justice at war's end. Undoubtedly, most were killed in the vicious fighting that took place, and given the meager numbers of Japanese prisoners, it seems likely most never answered, legally, for their crimes.

Cebu seemed to be an island with repeated Japanese atrocities. On Cebu, many of these incidents had surviving witnesses. A family of 11 was burned alive in their home by a group of Japanese soldiers.[166] People, entire families, disappeared, never to be seen again. Women were often pulled from homes and tortured and raped. At Tubog, the carnage was on a larger scale than those incidents previously illustrated. Chinese laborers and their families were "under suspicion" for guerilla activities. Thirty-three ci-

---

164 Theater Judge Advocate, *Murder, Attempted Murder, Torture and Attempted Rape of Civilians at Carcan, Cebu, P.I.* (General Headquarters: United States Army Forces, Pacific, Office Of The Theater Judge Advocate, War Crimes Branch, 1945), 1–2.

165 Theater Judge Advocate, *Murder of Two American Prisoners of War and Five Filipino Civilians on 26 March 1945, by Members of Japanese Kempei Tai* (General Headquarters: United States Army Forces, Pacific, Office Of The Theater Judge Advocate, War Crimes Branch, 1945), 1–4.

166 Theater Judge Advocate, *Murder of Palicte Family on or about 26 March 1945, Cebu City.* (General Headquarters: United States Army Forces, Pacific, Office Of The Theater Judge Advocate, War Crimes Branch, 1945), 1–6.

vilians were murdered (bayoneted, burned alive, raped and shot, thrown from the top floors of buildings).[167] Infants, three and six months old, were beaten to death. After this rampage, the Japanese set fire to multiple homes and left. Only the arrival of US troops saved the people from further Japanese barabarism.

A 105-mm howitzer being pulled by cable across a gorge. This is an example of how hard it was to get heavy weapons support to frontline troops on Mindanao.

---

167 Theater Judge Advocate, *Murder and Raping of Civilians and Burning of Civilian Homes at Tubog, Minglanilla, Cebu, P.I. on 30 and 31 January 1945* (General Headquarters: United States Army Forces, Pacific, Office Of The Theater Judge Advocate, War Crimes Branch, 1945), 1–2.

A US infantry squad in action on Sayre Highway. As is plainly obvious, this was a highway in name only. For most of its length, it amounted to little more than a gravel or mud-soaked path surrounded by dense jungle. Tank support was out of the question and air and artillery strikes had to be very precise to avoid inflicting friendly casualties.

VI

Opportunities for maneuver were few on Mindanao. The use of mechanized elements on most of the island was impossible because of the lack of roads and mobility of all troops was impeded further by stretches of marsh and thick jungle. These and other adverse features of the terrain complicated our combat operations, and our service troops were taxed to the utmost to overcome difficult problems of engineering, supply, communication, and medical evaluation.

—General Robert Eichelberger[168]

In this operation, the relative strength of friendly and enemy forces, the tremendous area involved, extensive distances negotiated, and the short time required to obtain a decisive victory, pay substantial tribute to the courage and aggressiveness of the combat soldier, and to the skill and superior devotion to duty of service troops participating.

—Foreword, History of X Corps
on Mindanao[169]

Thus far we have seen multiple Eighth Army operations in the Southern Philippines. All were limited to a single RCT or division, and other than vicious mop-up fighting after US forces had already consolidated their positions, none involved any type

---

168 Eighth Army, *Report Of The Commanding General On The Mindanao Operation, Victor V* (Headquarters: Eighth Army, 1945), 6.

169 X Corps, "Forward," in *History of X Corps on Mindanao* (Headquarters: X Corps, 1945).

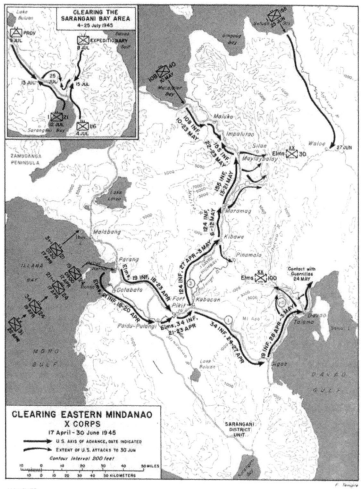

MAP 32

of operation that required a corps headquarters, let alone that of the entire Eighth Army. With the invasion of Mindanao, that all changed. Next to Luzon, Mindanao had the largest Japanese military force in the Philippines. As with the other islands attacked by the Eighth Army, it had no strategic purpose, as US forces already outflanked it. Further, the southern part of the island, the Zamboanga Peninsula, was already secure. But, as is abundantly clear with previous unnecessary operations, against the islands of

Panay, Negros, and Cebu, that did not matter militarily. General MacArthur would not ignore any Filipino territory occupied by the Japanese, especially when an enemy force of approximately 30-40,000 men inhabited the island. General Eichelberger assigned his X Corps (24th and 31st Infantry Divisions) the task of invading and securing Mindanao.

The 24th and 31st Infantry Division's fought their own separate campaigns within the larger campaign on Mindanao. The 24th landed first, at Parang, on April 17, and drove east for Davao. The 31st followed the 24th, moving east to Kabacan before driving north. Other units (segments of the 40th and 41st Infantry Divisions) also participated in this operation, but in minor combat and support roles. The main routes of the march were dictated by Mindanao's mountainous terrain, as it dominated the island. The roads that moved between these heights, which gave the Japanese a definitive defensive advantage, were, along with the various rivers and streams, the only possible routes of advance. Overland movement was not an option. The island's many bridges were obvious choke points and the Japanese several times during the course of the campaign held up the US advance by destroying those bridges. The 24th and 31st Infantry Divisions never launched coordinated attacks during the campaign, so each is examined separately.

The Japanese on Mindanao were formidable in number: it was the second largest force in the Philippines, but essentially mediocre in capability. They possessed few heavy weapons, little to no transport, no air support, and an ever-dwindling supply of food, ammunition, and medical supplies (which at this point in the war made them no different than any other Japanese force). An initial estimate of Japanese strength on Mindanao, according to Eighth Army Intelligence, was approximately 30,000 troops.[170] The Japanese units were:

---

170 Eighth Army, *Report Of The Commanding General On The Mindanao Operation, Victor V,* 14.

The campaign for Mindanao was limited due to the thick, mountainous terrain of the island. The 24th Infantry Division drove east from its original landing at Parang, toward Davao. The 31st landed at Parang several days later, drove east, and then headed north, where they trapped Japanese forces along the Sayre Highway.

The principal combat units in central and eastern Mindanao were the 100th Division and the remaining elements of the 30th Division. The former had an estimated effective strength of 8,000 .... The 30th Division ... its effective strength had been reduced by the transfer of certain elements mostly infantry to Leyte. The remaining infantry units, plus artillery and other divisional units, gave the division an estimated strength of 7,000.

Although the enemy's force was of considerable size, it was spread over a large area. Lack of transportation, the poor condition of the roads, and the restrictions on daytime movement imposed by the threat of air attacks would make it impossible for the enemy to concentrate his forces at any point where we might attack. Therefore, it was expected that the enemy could be defeated in detail, in approximately the areas where he was deployed at the beginning of the operation. The largest concentration was known to be in the Davao area, where the principal elements of the 100th Division were located with enough naval base and service troops to make a total of 15,500 for the Davao Gulf area.[171]

---

171 *Ibid.,* 15–16.

These numbers were largely the work of the island's guerilla units. After major operations ended and mopping up occurred during July and August, it was discovered that the initial estimates of 30,000 Japanese on Mindanao was massively wrong. The number at war's end was raised to 50,000, although most of that difference in number was scattered amongst the island's many mountains and never operated in a cohesive fashion.

Guerillas have been mentioned throughout this examination. On Mindanao, they also played a prominent role. The island itself aided these units in the war against the Japanese. The Army General Headquarters, SWPA, noted:

> The guerilla resistance movement in Mindanao is unique in several respects. The movement was guided and directly mainly by Americans; it organized shortly after the surrender of USAFFE forces; it was quickly supplied with arms and ammunition from SWPA, it developed a civil administration parallel with its military organization, and in every respect justified the confidence of the US in the loyalty of the Filipino people.

> Conditions in Mindanao were favorable to the formation of a guerilla movement. A comparatively large number of Americans, both military and civilian, were available for such work.

> There were few casualties among Filipino military and civilian leaders, most of whom cooperated with the guerillas. The island was large in area, with numerous isolated food producing sections and extremely limited road nets. The cities (which the enemy occupied) were all on the coast—Davao, Cotabato, Zamboanga, Cagayan, and Surigao. The enemy listed his ac-

tivities to control of the cities and patrol of road
nets and waterways. The hinterland, comprising
ninety-five percent of the island, was free of enemy occupation or patrols. In effect, Mindanao,
throughout the period following the surrender
of USAFFE forces in May 1942, was ninety-five
percent American territory with "Japanese guerillas" occupying a few coastal cities.[172]

The Army's official campaign also notes before the main landings
even happened that:

The guerillas had added greatly to the woes of
Morozumi and Harada (the Japanese division
commanders) by April 1945. For example, the
Japanese transportation problems were many
times compounded by guerilla demolitions,
roadblocks, and bridge destruction. Guerilla
raids had destroyed communications equipment
and supply dumps. It was impossible for the Japanese to send small truck convoys up and down
the roads of eastern Mindanao, and small patrols
had been out of the question for months.[173]

When the campaign ended, the X Corps official history noted
that "the guerilla forces on Mindanao contributed materially to
the success of the campaign."[174] Nowhere was that more evident
than on April 17, the day of the initial landing.

Malabang, on Mindanao's western coast, was the objective of the
initial landings. The town itself and a nearby airfield was secured
by the island's guerilas, offering an opportunity to land further
south at Parang, where the 24th, which landed first, could advance quickly along Route 1 toward Fort Pikit. The landings were

---

172 *The Guerilla Resistance Movement In The Philippines*, 83.

173 Smith, 623.

174 X Corps, *History of X Corps on Mindanao*, 64.

easy and virtually unopposed. Six Japanese soldiers were killed and only 2 US soldiers wounded.[175] The 24th then drove east. At this point, a familiar pattern developed. US units would advance, sometimes stopping due to stubborn resistance, which would be pounded by artillery and or air power (often using the new napalm), or to bridges having been destroyed by the Japanese. The advance would continue, casualties would increase, but never enough to stop operations. Within two weeks, the 24th was within 10 miles of Davao, the campaign's ultimate objective.

Although the 24th Infantry Division crossed Mindanao in about two weeks, it was in no manner an easy movement. The division's history, specifically referring to its 19th Regimental Combat Team, notes that it:

> completed a long and arduous movement involving an overland march of forty-two miles under the most trying conditions. The road twisted and turned through hills and expanses of cogon grass which had overgrown the highway. The heat had been almost unbearable and the lack of motor transportation had put the burden of hand carrying on the first troops for the entire distance. There were many heat prostrations all along the way. The 1st Battalion made the whole march on foot. Five enemy trucks, three of which were booby-trapped, were captured and put into shuttle use for the other battalions.[176]

Heat, jungle, inferior roads. All common obstacles faced by US soldiers in the Southwest Pacific. The only major battle in this first part of the campaign happened at Digos, a town in close proximity to Mindanao's eastern coast and approximately 30

---

175 Eighth Army, *Report Of The Commanding General On The Mindanao Operation, Victor V,* 25.

176 24th Infantry Division, *Mindanao: Historical Report of the 24th Infantry Division* (Headquarters: 24th Infantry Division, 1945), 8.

miles south of Davao. Attacks failed in the face of Japanese small arms fire. Pillboxes brilliantly camouflaged by the island's high grass frustrated another attack, enemy artillery fire still another. An air attack failed to break the stalemate, but another air strike, this time employing napalm, cleared away most of the forbidding jungle, burnt the Japanese out of their caves and pillboxes, and allowed the division to reach Digos. General Woodruff, the 24th division commander, praised the efforts of his men:

> I am very proud of my men and officers. I think the division has accomplished a feat which, I frankly confess, I thought in the beginning to be nearly impossible.

> We came through fast. We refused to see Japs behind every tree. We caught them expecting an attack from the other way, disorganized them and kept them that way.

> The men are tired but they are ready for whatever may lie ahead of them.[177]

Worthy praise and at the same time, remarkably accurate as a future forecast. The hardest fighting of the campaign now began.

With Digos in US hands, Mindanao was essentially cut in half and Japanese forces were left in isolated pockets, although those pockets still had to be eliminated. For the 24th Infantry Division, Davao remained the main objective. It had a port, several nearby airfields, and most of what was left of the Japanese 100th Division. To capture Davao the 24th first had to secure Hill 500, which:

> commanded all approaches to Davao City, the steep-sided hill mass ... was the key to the defense of the former naval base and hemp metropolis of the world. The hill was fortified with ev-

---

177 *Ibid.*, 16.

ery type of Japanese armament, and the fortifi-
cations, built during three years of preparation
against attack extended northward over the entire area in a depth of some 3,000 yards.

Automatic weapons covered every approach ....
The slopes were terraced with emplacements,
machine guns of all calibers, anti-aircraft guns
firing explosive shells at flat trajectory, naval
guns embedded in concrete, and rockets impro-
vised from aerial bombs.[178]

There is something vital to be taken from the above. The Japanese expected an attack against Davao directly from the sea. That
is what their most elaborate preparations focused on. The 24th's
drive through the center of Mindanao and turn to approach the
city from the south allowed US units to enter the Davao area
against disorganized, moderate opposition.[179] The fight for the
city was brutal. Manila had been destroyed several months earlier and hundreds of thousands of civilians had been killed. While
not on the scale of Manila, Davao was also destroyed and many
of its people were killed.

For 17 days, attacks in and around Davao proceeded. The 24th
Infantry Division's 19th RCT launched an attack on May 10. The
attack was repulsed. Heavy artillery and air support preceded a
May 11 attack. It too failed. May 12 was a day of reconnaissance
as the US attempted to pinpoint the exact Japanese positions. It
did little good, as Japanese mortar and artillery fire stopped the
attack of May 13. May 14 was more of the same. By May 19, the
hill was finally taken, as Japanese positions were methodically destroyed by artillery and air strikes, infantry armed with explosives
and flamethrowers, and vicious hand-to-hand fighting. Isolated

---

178 Ibid., 26.

179 21st Infantry Regiment, *Mindanao: A Regiment In Action* (Headquarters:
21st Infantry Regiment, 1945), 122–23.

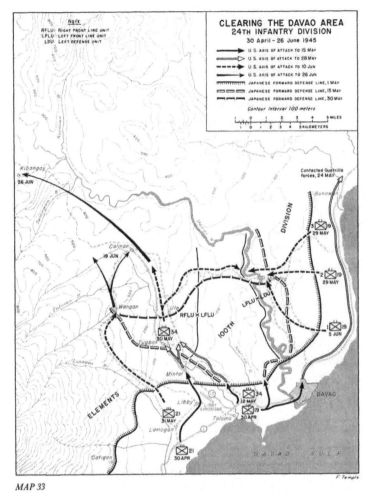

MAP 33

The final attack on Davao

Japanese continued to fight on in the 19th RCT's sector, but by May 22, it was over.[180]

The 34th Regimental Combat Team of the 24th Infantry Division also faced a continuously frustrating tactical situation. The Regiment's official history notes:

180 Eighth Army, *Report Of The Commanding General On The Mindanao Operation, Victor V,* 50–52.

Hillside and ridge-top pillboxes had been the chief obstacles of the Hill 500 engagement. Indirect artillery fire had been having good effect on the general defensive dispositions of the enemy, but had been leaving these pillboxes untouched in many cases. The same was true of air strikes. Moreover, the process of bringing fire on the bunkers had a retarding effect on the operation. An attacking unit, coming upon a strongpoint was forced to withdraw to safety limits before supporting fire could be brought to bear. The terrain was precipitous and movement over it difficult. Each target had to be registered in separately. The whole process was unsatisfactory.[181]

The solution? Direct fire from 90-mm anti-aircraft guns and self-propelled howitzers. These weapons were brought to the infantry and as they advanced, they could observe and cover their movements. This had previously been next to impossible due to the jungle and mountainous terrain, but all efforts were made to bring this support forward. At minimal distances, Japanese pillboxes were quickly eliminated. The city was then taken, but at an exorbitant cost.

Davao was destroyed. US bombing had done considerable damage to the city and the 24th stated over 99% of Davao was destroyed.[182] The Japanese had taken anything they could from the city, with little regard for its inhabitants. Japanese brutality is only sparingly referred to in the official US reports of these campaigns. It did not factor into the planning and conduct of operations, but after seeing the final paragraph of the 24th's historical report, maybe it should have been. They observed:

---

181 34th Infantry Regiment, *Historical Report Of The Mindanao Operation, 17 April–7 July 1945, 21* (Headquarters: 34th Infantry Regiment, 1945).

182 24th Infantry Division, *Mindanao: Historical Report of the 24th Infantry Division,* 30.

Not many days after its capture, thousands of Filipinos straggled into Davao, a sick, famished, terrified horde. Madame Baldamera Sexan, the director of Davao's Mission Hospital, testified that some 25,000 Filipinos had died through starvation, disease, and murder during Japanese rule. During later stages of the campaign, the Jap military embarked on an orgy of rape and murder which virtually exterminated the inhabitants of five outlying communities.[183]

This is examined in later pages because the suffering of the Filipino people at the hands of their Japanese occupiers is a story that must be told.

The 19th and 34th were the principal regiments in the Davao fighting, but the 21st Regimental Combat Team, the third of the 24th Infantry Division's infantry regiments, was also involved in the general campaign to that point. Between the time of landing on April 17 and 30, the 21st had a relatively easy time of it. They met little opposition, in fact experiencing no enemy contact between April 23 and 26.[184] Unlike the 19th and 34th, the 21st RCT made its first major movements by water, moving down the Mindanao River to the junctions of Routes 1 and 5.[185] The regiment landed and began their overland march.

The first few days of May saw sporadic action, with small losses to both the regiment and the enemy. On May 3, the regiment captured Mintal, a town from which most of its operations over the course of the next month would originate. On May 5, the first real opposition was encountered at the Talomo River. A heavy fight against entrenched Japanese with plenty of artillery support

---

183 *Ibid.*

184 21st Infantry Regiment, *Report After Combat: 21st Infantry Regiment, 17 April–30 June 45* (Headquarters: 21st Infantry Regiment, 1945), 5.

185 *Ibid.,* 5–7.

(47-, 75-, and 90-mm guns) resulted in 47 enemy killed and 27 US casualties, despite heavy artillery and air support and even the help of three tanks. The ease of the landing and initial advances became bitter fights and the regiment moved into the island's interior.

May 6–7 saw 125 enemy dead and 61 US casualties as the Japanese from the heights poured fire down on troops dealing with the jungle and numerous Japanese pillboxes. May 8 saw 73 US dead and wounded; 38 enemy dead were found, although there were undoubtedly more buried in caves or hidden in the jungle. May 9 again saw more total US casualties than confirmed Japanese dead: 56 US dead and wounded and 46 Japanese dead. These numbers are what the war in the Philippines had become. The Japanese occupied strong positions, but had no hope of support or resupply. They had to fight and survive with what they had; surrender was not an option until war's end. The only way the Japanese positions were relevant was if Americans attacked them. Every attack made an irrelevant force matter, and although the Japanese were already defeated, US losses continued to grow. Nevertheless, the advances continued. May 10 was a day of consolidation and patrolling, while May 11 saw a rarity at this point in the war: a Japanese attack of over 100 men. It was easily repulsed. US losses were 12 killed and wounded; Japanese losses were 53 dead. Until May 17, other than patrolling, there was little US action. On May 18 and 19, the regiment attacked and seized the town of Tugbok. May 20–21 saw the clearing of the town and heavy fighting, resulting in 103 Japanese dead and 14 US casualties. May 22–24 saw stiff resistance in sporadic engagements, while May 25 saw another Japanese attack and 41 more of the enemy dead. The rest of May involved days of patrolling and minor contacts. June, with the exception of a few vicious battles, was more of the same, patrolling and minor contacts. The regiment and the entire 24th Infantry Division were relieved on June 30. The 21st had killed 2,133 Japanese soldiers, taken 14 prisoners, and sustained approximately 900 casualties in almost three months of action.[186]

For the 19th and 34th Regimental Combat Teams, the fighting did not end with the fall of Davao. The 19th moved on Mandog, an area where a small Japanese garrison resided and those fleeing the city were concentrated. Progress for the 19th was good. In fact on May 29, they advanced 3,000 yards, an unheard of gain once the heavy fighting began after the initial push across the island.[187] Resistance was of course fierce, but the Air Force's new weapon, napalm, continued to work. After the large gains of May 29, progress was slower as Japanese artillery and rocket fire continued. Napalm and artillery fire ended the enemy fire and the Japanese found themselves essentially trapped. The Eighth Army noted:

> The enemy was now boxed in but had no intention of giving up without a fight. During the next ten days the American forces were subjected continuously to mortar and artillery fire. Additional difficulties were caused by rains, which came down almost continuously and landslides that were started by electrically detonated mines. The defenders in the caves around the area, frequently resisted until the caves were blown in on top of them, while others made almost nightly counterattacks. During the action, air and artillery support, the regimental cannon, and the battalion mortars were used to the maxim.[188]

Again, US units attacking the Japanese in these conditions and under these circumstances inevitably led to the enemy's destruction, but US losses also continued to rise. It was hard, dirty work

---

186 *Ibid.,* 7–10.

187 Eighth Army, *Report Of The Commanding General On The Mindanao Operation, Victor V,* 57.

188 *Ibid.,* 58.

made far more difficult by Mindanao's mountainous topography and overgrown jungle. All attacks had to be made along the island's few roads and the ingenuous Japanese:

> built innumerable pillboxes and a very elaborate system of trenches, foxholes, and spider holes. Not only had these been camouflaged by the Japanese, but by natural growth as well. It was quite often impossible to detect these emplacements when only a few feet from them. Full advantage had been taken of the dense abaca groves. Due to the denseness of the surrounding vegetation and intense heat, movement off the roads was very limited.[189]

This was what US forces faced throughout the island. The 34th RCT spent most of its time after Hill 550 and Davao in a fight for what its troops called Pushback Hill.

The Japanese, after the loss of Davao, hastily prepared a new defensive line in the vicinity of the Bancal-Mintal Road. The 34th began their operation on May 10, making little progress for the first four days against the usual heavy Japanese rifle and automatic weapons fire. Even tank destroyers, usually reliable and impervious to enemy fire, withdrew because their accompanying infantry drew so much attention. May 14-20 again saw little progress, but the objective, Pushback Hill, was but a few hundred yards away. There, the advance stopped. As per normal, the Japanese were well entrenched, well camouflaged, and firing everything they had. Tank support arrived for a multi-company attack on the 21st. A quick mortar and artillery barrage preceded the attack. The previous afternoon, the 34th had pulled back a few hundred yards to consolidate their lines. This attack seemed to be going well until reaching the same point where the prior attack was stopped. Japanese pillboxes on both sides of the road caught the advancing troops in a murderous crossfire and the road was

---

189 21st Infantry Regiment, *Mindanao: A Regiment In Action*, 126.

not wide or sturdy enough for the tanks to advance enough to engage. The halted troops then received Japanese mortar fire. A quick withdrawal began so air support could join the fray.

Late in the afternoon, an air strike of napalm and strafing runs hit the Japanese. Scant minutes later, 17 more planes arrived with high explosive bombs, dropping them a few hundred yards from friendly troops. As patrols preceding the main attack moved forward, they found 65 Japanese bodies, but a resilient enemy still remained and their fire drove the patrols back. On the 22nd, a battalion launched a double envelopment of the Japanese position behind a "rolling" artillery barrage.

One hundred and fifty yards short of the objective fire from everything, the Japanese had hit. For several hours, the fight continued and with no progress made and casualties mounting, the US troops once again pulled back.[190]

Heavier support for another attack on May 24 was hoped to be enough to break the stalemate. Four separate air strikes, utilizing napalm, high explosive bombs, and follow-up strafing runs, pounded the Japanese. At midday, they were joined by three battalions of artillery (105-mm and 155-mm howitzers). Two of the 34th's three infantry battalions advanced immediately after the cessation of the artillery fire. Heavy air and artillery support still were not enough.[191]

On the morning of May 25, every gun and plane available hit Pushback Hill. The two battalions again advanced and this time secured the hill. The only remaining Japanese were dead. The 34th spent the rest of May consolidating their gains and most of June patrolling and encountering only minor contact. The regiment's two months on Mindanao were both successful and costly. They attained their objectives and killed 2,405 Japanese soldiers. US losses in this regiment were 141 killed, 675 wounded,

---

190 34th Infantry Regiment, *Historical Report Of The Mindanao Operation, 17 April–7 July 1945*, 24–25.

191 *Ibid.*, 25–29.

and 1,900 non-battle and "battle-induced" casualties, the result of prolonged combat in a jungle environment against a fanatical enemy.[192] The other part of the Eighth Army's X Corps, the 31st Infantry Division, also played a significant role in the conquest of Mindanao.

The 31st made its greatest mark on its drive north up Sayre Highway. It made its initial landing several days after the 24th and moved east to the junction of Route 1 and Sayre Highway. The Japanese once again made a serious error ascertaining US intentions. The Japanese set up their defenses at Davao expecting an attack from the sea and the 24th Infantry Division's drive from the west and south had caught them unprepared. With the Sayre Highway, the Japanese expected any attack would happen after an amphibious landing at Macajalar Bay. The 24th had primarily fought the Japanese 100th Division. The 31st dealt with the enemy's 30th Division, a conglomeration of approximately 17,500 men scattered amongst the northern half of the island.[193] This strength was dispersed as follows:

1. Kabacan north to Kibawe – 2,500 men (infantry with a mix of other units)

2. Kibawe to Maluko – 5,500 men (infantry and headquarters/division units)

3. Macajalar Bay Area – 4,500 men (conglomeration of all types of units and specialties)

4. Butuan Bay – 2,200 men (infantry)

Given Japan's lack of transport units, such as the one at Butuan Bay, could not be brought west to help any of the other scattered commands of the 30th Division. Each part of the enemy command was a bastion onto itself, able to fight on as long as possible with what they had, but also knowing they could expect no help

---

192 *Ibid.*, 29.

193 Smith, 636.

from nor provide help to sister units. For this paralysis, much of the credit has to be given to Mindanao's guerillas. The Japanese force at Butuan Bay was in all respects besieged since Filipino guerillas had blocked every road and destroyed every bridge available to them.[194] Sayre Highway itself was also a highway in name only. It was falling apart because the Japanese had done nothing to improve it and was overgrown with jungle. The Japanese would build a bridge and the guerillas would destroy it. Even at night, the only time of day the Japanese were free of the harassment of US air attacks, the guerillas picked up the slack. Once again, the Filipinos proved their value indirectly to a campaign.

Of the 31st Infantry Division's three RCTs (124th, 155th, 167th), the 124th made the initial push north on April 27. Initial movements were relatively easy until a point approximately eight miles north of Kabacan, where the regiment had a typical bitter battle with the enemy, only this one was at night. The division history notes:

> Less than eight miles northward from Kabacan the battalion engaged the enemy in a battle lasting from 2200I to the withdrawal of the opposing force at dawn. This initial encounter with the enemy force advancing southward occurred with the leading elements in a defile. The low swampy ground prevented flanking and enveloping movements. With these leading elements engaging the enemy, the battalion deployed and rapidly took up a position on rising ground astride the highway immediately south of the defile, covered with dense, head-high cogon grass. Batteries B and C, 149th F.A. Bn, quickly moved into positions and delivered continuous, accurate fire through the night. Contact was maintained by sporadic exchanges of rifle

---

194 *Ibid.*, 637.

and mortar fire and skirmishes with small enemy detachments until shortly after 0100I when
the enemy began the first of a series of "banzai"
attacks. Against the repeated fanatical attacks,
the battalion engaged in furious close quarter
and hand to hand fighting until dawn, when
the decimated, thoroughly disorganized enemy
force was routed and dispersed in the dense terrain to the north. This action is noteworthy in
that it is believed to be the first night meeting
engagement in the SWPA operations in which a
sizeable force participated in and the action was
fought to a decision.[195]

While historic, most of the other days in the division's movements toward the initial push up Sayre Highway were fast and
without protracted battles. The major impediment facing the
31st was supply problems and that resulted from Mindanao's forbidding terrain. Blown bridges were everywhere on the highway.
Some destroyed by the Japanese, others by Filipino guerillas at-
tempting to frustrate the Japanese. All it did was frustrate the US
advance. Constant rain and enormous gorges and ravines forced
ingenuity on an incredible scale in order to provide heavy weapons support and basic supplies. Nature was also the enemy:

Terrain and weather played an increasingly important role to delay our forces. The majority of
the bridges along the Highway had either been
destroyed or were of fragile construction which
would not support greater than ¾ ton vehicles.
In many cases it was impossible to bypass the
bridges because of impassable terrain adjacent
to the road. Almost nightly precipitation rendered the main supply route impassable; sup-

---

195 31st Infantry Division, *Operations Report: Mindanao* (Headquarters: 31st
Infantry Division, 1945), 22.

plies, heavy equipment and artillery pieces were held up at the Mulita River some thirty miles to the rear, which necessitated drops by air to the leading elements. The mountainous terrain presented a great hazzard for pilots striving to locate identifying panels in the dense growth below. Drops were limited to bare necessities—food, ammunition and medical supplies.[196]

The impact of nature was quite apparent in the 124th's fight in the Battle of Colgan Woods, so named in honor of chaplain Thomas A. Colgan, who was killed helping wounded in the dense jungle. The battle took six days because of the arduous task of gathering enough support to launch a successful attack. Initially, the infantry only had their 4.2 inch mortars for fire support (the weapons and their ammunition having to be carried by hand into position) and sporadic air strikes. The 124th was reluctant to employ heavy air strikes because of the close proximity of the enemy to their own positions and the difficulty locating the Japanese in the thick jungle. By the end of those six days, artillery and other vital supplies were finally in position. The mortars, artillery, and dive bombers (able to deliver bombs with greater accuracy than mass air strikes) broke the Japanese resistance and the 124th secured the Colgan Woods, although it took a few more days of "mopping up."[197]

The 155th Regimental Combat Team faced similar problems with both nature and the Japanese along the Pulangi River. Vehicles that had managed to drag artillery forward were stranded for lack of fuel and the guns were often silent for lack of ammunition. The Japanese were "dug-in behind protecting and camouflaging tree roots on the steep slopes of the ridges. Positions were well constructed and prepared in depth and in many cases could not be flanked."[198] How did the 155th overcome their supply prob-

---

196 *Ibid.,* 25.

197 *Ibid.,* 25–27.

198 *Ibid.,* 33.

lems? For fuel, they floated 55-gallon steel drums down the river. For ammunition, small rubber boats did the trick. Both these ideas helped, although they could not completely solve the supply problems. Over a period of several days, enough food, fuel, and ammunition accumulated to support the attack. For four days, constant fire and attacks made little progress. Flamethrowers finally burnt the enemy from their positions within the massive trees.[199]

Such was the remainder of the Mindanao campaign. There were small, vicious fights in isolated spots, but for the most part, the 31st Infantry Division drove north. They were aided by the 40th Infantry Division's 108th Infantry Regiment, which had landed at Macanjar Bay and drove south, catching the Japanese in a vice and forcing them to scatter in the mountainous jungle to the east and west of Sayre Highway. Thousands of Japanese soldiers remained there until the end of the war. The 108th's only major fight began on May 13 on its approach to the entrance to Mangina Canyon. The Japanese defenses:

> covered both flanks of the entrance to the canyon, and patrols reconnoitering the area discovered that the canyon itself was strongly defended. Weapons of every caliber from small arms to heavy artillery, were strategically emplaced and well camouflaged, commanding every approach with registered fire. Many barbed wire installations and mines attached to trip wires had been set up.[200]

It took until May 18 before the Japanese pillboxes and other positions were finally eliminated.

The 167th Regimental Combat Team's advance was quick until

---

199 155th Infantry Regiment, *History: Mindanao, April–June 1945* (Headquarters: 155th Infantry Regiment, 1945), 9–11.

200 Smith, 639.

it reached a crossing of the Pulangi River at Sanipon on May 13. Here the Japanese "had prepared strong defensive positions on the hills and both sides of the river. Slopes of the hills had been blown over the roads in places, and the road was mined. The Japanese were well-equipped with machine guns, 90-mm mortars, and small arms. Intense fire was received from a steep cliff to the southwest."[201] The Regiment's 3rd Battalion then spent ten days slogging through Japanese defenses. Eventually two battalions were able to outflank the village, cross the river, and destroy any remaining foeces in the area.

With the two main Japanese forces on Mindanao broken, the 30th Division along Sayre Highway by the 31st Infantry Division and the 100th Division by the 24th Infantry Division at Davao, mopping up was all that remained. As seen throughout this history, that could be slow and dangerous. The Army's official historian of the entire Philippines Campaign, Robert Ross Smith, put it best:

> With Sayre Highway cleared of the 30th Division and with the collapse of the 100th Division second line of defense northwest of Davao, the campaign for eastern Mindanao had reached a tactical conclusion. However, as was the case on most of the other islands of the philippines, the war was not over in eastern Mindanao X Corps operations now entered the mop-up and pursuit phase.[202]

As the war entered its final months, the US forces moved rapidly but the Japanese just retreated faster. By June 30, General Eichelberger considered the campaign over. US losses on Mindanao were the heaviest the Eighth Army suffered during the Southern Philippines campaign. A total of 820 men were killed and another 2,880 were wounded.[203] Japanese losses were both heavy and

---

201 Eighth Army, *Report Of The Commanding General On The Mindanao Operation, Victor V,* 67.

202 Smith, 642.

203 *Ibid.,* 648.

surprising. Depending on which command's estimates of enemy strength one finds the most reliable, the Japanese had anywhere from 30,000 to 50,000 personnel on Mindanao. US and guerilla action accounted for 12,865 Japanese and prisoners by June 30. At war's end, 22,250 Japanese soldiers and over 11,000 civilians came from the mountains.[204] That leaves several thousands more unaccounted for, most likely casualties of starvation, disease, and exposure. Far more Japanese troops survived the war than were killed by the Eighth Army, but they were unable to impact US operations.

Mindanao also saw its share of abuse at the hands of the Japanese. During one horrible month (May 19–June 15, 1945) before US forces reached them, the small towns of Ilang-Ilang and Bunawan saw dozens mudered and many more taken, never to be seen again. Japanese soldiers dragged a 13-member family from their home, tied them to trees, and bayoneted them. Others were dragged out and beheaded, including several infants. A mass shooting occurred on June 14, 1945, where approximately 200 were killed. Children were starved. The toll on these towns may have surpassed 1,000 innocent people.[205] In Davao City, before the arrival of the 24th Infantry Division, the Japanese exacted a price from the city's inhabitants. A family and its neighbors, 34 people in all, were herded into an air raid shelter. The women were repeatedly raped and then bunched together; several grenades were thrown into the mass of people. Any survivors were then shot.[206] Other families were attacked randomly and shot; any survivors, including infants and young children, were bayo-

---

204 All enemy numbers. *Ibid.,* 649.

205 Theater Judge Advocate, *Murders at Ilang-Ilang and Bunawan, Davao, Mindanao, P.I., between 14 May and 15 June 1945* (General Headquarters: United States Army Forces, Pacific, Office of the Theater Judge Advocate, War Crimes Branch, 1946), 1–5.

206 Theater Judge Advocate, *Murder and Rape of Filipino Civilians in Davao City, Mindanao, P.I. in May 1945* (General Headquarters: United States Army Forces, Pacific, Office Of The Theater Judge Advocate, War Crimes Branch, 1946), 1.

neted. Hundreds were maimed or murdered. The vicious cycle throughout the Southern Philippines continued until Americans liberated them. As previously stated, this work is an examination of the military history of the Eighth Army. These campaigns made little sense tactically or strategically. Morally, it made complete sense; however, that morality never entered the equation for why these operations took place. It should have. The examples put forward in these last few pages clearly demonstrate that. MacArthur had to know what was going on here. Emotion is not supposed to enter the equation when determining military strategy and if MacArthur had told President Roosevelt that helping the Filipino people was his main objective, Admiral Nimitz's strategic argument for devoting all resources into a Central Pacific drive would have made military sense. The military and honor restoring value of the Philippines allowed it to be included in the greater Pacific strategy. MacArthur's staff was in contact with Filipino guerillas on these islands. They knew what was going on. Perhaps MacArthur's insistence to regain ALL the Philippines had a deeper motive. It is at this point conjecture, but it does suggest his strategy concerning the Philippines be reexamined.

General Eichelberger was very pleased with the performance of the X Corps' 24th and 31st Infantry Divisions during this campaign. He addressed all his commands and then the X Corps specifically:

> I give great credit to the able, skillful and determined leadership of my senior commanders, Major Franklin C. Sibert, X Corps, Major General Roscoe B. Woodruff, 24th Infantry Division, Major General Clarence A. Martin, 31st Infantry Division, Brigadier General Robert O. Shoe and Lieutenant Colonel Marcus D. Stratta, 108th Regimental Combat Team, and Colonel Harold M. Lindstrom, 162nd Regimental Combat Team, whose respective commands all

participated admirably in the complex and wide-spread operations.[207]

To General Sibert he stated:

> Please extend to the officers and men of your command my heartiest congratulations on the successful completion of the mission assigned for Victor – 5. Despite difficult terrain, bad weather, the campaign progressed at a rapid rate and the officers and men by their vigorous prosecution of combat were able to rapidly disintegrate one of the largest forces remaining in the philippines. A good job well done.[208]

With the close of fighting on Mindanao, the Eighth Army had one more mission in the Pacific War.

---

207 124th Infantry Regiment, *Historical Record of the Mindanao Campaign* (Headquarters: 124th Infantry Regiment, 1945), 31–32.

208 *Ibid.*

VII

The final chapter of the long and savagely fought campaign of Luzon has been written. Since 9 January 1945 when the assault landing was made in Lingayen Gulf, elements of the Division have been activly committed in combat. It is believed that this record of 219 days continuous action is unsurpassed in th Pacific War. The action has been bloody and our losses severe. It is to our immortal dead, rather than to us the living, that we owe our success in arms.

—C.E. Hurdis, Major General,
US Army Commanding, Sixth Infantry Division

The Eighth Army began its existence as the mop-up force on Leyte, finishing off scattered Japanese units left over from the Sixth Army. They ended their role in WWII on Luzon, once again mopping up for the Sixth Army. the Eighth Army was also reorganized, taking on several former Sixth Army divisions as they sought to clear the vast territory in northern Luzon. The divisions that landed on Negros, Cebu, and Mindanao remained there, refitting and preparing for the anticipated invasion of Japan. The Sixth, 32nd, and 38th Infantry Divisions now came under Eighth Army control. They were tired, depleted, and looking forward to war's end. Protracted battles were something these divisions hoped to avoid. The Japanese were no longer the enemy of the early months of the Philippines campaign. A protracted fight was now beyond their capabilities.

The Sixth Infantry Division was responsible for the area around Kiangan and Bontoc and its 12-15,000 Japanese soldiers.[209] The

209 Sixth Infantry Division, *After Action Report: Final Phase Of Luzon Cam-*

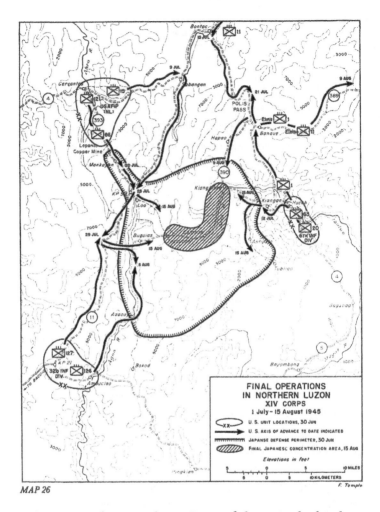

MAP 26

Sixth spent its first months on Luzon fighting in the harsh terrain around the Wawa and Ipo Dams. In this area it was no better. From July 1-8, the Battle for Lane's Ridge, its first battle, lasted eight days; three of those days were spent clearing a landslide on a key highway.[210] Opposition was brushed aside or destroyed with artillery fire and air power, infantry conducted methodical

---

paign, *1 July To 21 August 1945* (Headquarters: Sixth Infantry Division, 1945), 2.

210 *Ibid.*

rather than rapid advances. On July 5, a hail of Japanese small arms fire stopped the advance. On July 7, a heavy air strike utilizing napalm silenced the ridge. A more capable enemy at this point in the war could have seriously stymied the US advance. The ridge: "was later found to consist of 55 mutually supporting emplacements, including 13 pillboxes and 22 caves, with enemy riflemen and machine gunners well dug in. The position selected could only be assaulted frontally, as the flanks were protected by almost impenetrable undergrowth and deep ravines."[211] One hundred and fifty Japanese dead were discovered.

Lane's Ridge was the exception rather than the rule. Nature, not the Japanese, was the biggest threat. Along Highway 4, a key transportation artery, vehicles were stranded for days by floods, entire platoons were engulfed by water and marooned, air supply was made impossible by the constant rains, rock and mud slides were all along the highway, etc., etc., etc. Engineers worked constantly, and it was dangerous work: snipers, land mines, and of course nature. The advance continued. By July 24, the Sixth's 63rd Infantry Regiment, the primary force in this part of the campaign had casualties of 48 killed and 195 wounded. Japanese losses were 2,383 killed and 119 prosoners.[212]

The Sixth's 20th Infantry Regiment spent the rest of the war in Luzon's Cagayan Valley. They began their advance on July 5. There were several quick fights, but nothing held up the advance until July 16, when weather stopped everything for five days. When the advance resumed, the ground was treacherous and support unable to follow. Nevertheless, by July 23, the 20th had killed 382 Japanese soldiers and taken 207 prisoners. US losses were two killed and 15 wounded.[213]

The last of the Sixth Infantry Division's "big fights" occurred in August at a ridge defended by approximately 100 enemy soldiers.

---

211 *Ibid.,* 3.

212 *Ibid.,* 6–7.

213 *Ibid.,* 10.

The Japanese:

> transformed this ridge line and reverse slop
> into a veritable fortress, bristling with automat-
> ic weapons, organized in depth and excellently
> camouflaged against air and ground observa-
> tion. On the crest of the ridge, the enemy had
> constructed numerous caves which were con-
> nected by tunnels. Spider holes were also dug
> on the military crest an the reverse slope. Many
> of these holes had underground connecting tun-
> nels. The extremely precitpitous approaches to
> the top of the ridge made it difficult to assault.
> Some idea of how difficult is shown by the fact
> that it took two hours for troops to scale the al-
> most vertical slopes.[214]

How did the 20th deal with this position? Lots of firepower. Before the infantry reached the ridge it was hit with:

1. Artillery – 4,000 rounds
2. 4.2 inch mortars – 8,000 rounds
3. 81-mm mortars – 8,000 rounds
4. Nine tons of high explosive bombs
5. 26,000 gallons of napalm[215]

The ridge was easily taken. Mt. Puloy was another point much like
the above that also could have required an exorbinant amount of
firepower to reduce and even a possible infantry assault. It never
came to be. The war ended before the attack commenced.

In the Southern Cordillera Central Mountains, 18,000 Japanese
troops under the direction of General Tomoyuli Yamashita, the
commander of all enemy units in the Philippines, were concentrated. The US objective was to tighten the noose around these

214 *Ibid.,* 20.
215 *Ibid.*

men, prevent their escape, and then destroy them. The Sixth Infantry Division, with Filipino support, conducted most of the operations here. The terrain was marked by steep cliffs, heavy jungle, and frequent landslides, which were made all the worse by incessant heavy rains. From July 1-12, there were frequent fights, but US artillery and air power did most of the work, killing 1,699 Japanese soldiers and taking 167 prisoners.[216]

While the Sixth continued its active patrolling and sporadic fights, including a foolish Japanese night attack on US positions in the Banki area that cost them over 600 dead, the Filipino continued to enter the fight.[217] Facing prepared Japanese positions, they attacked at Mankayan, Sabangan, and Bontoc. US artillery and air support was always there. In one bitter fight, the 66th Filipino Infantry Regiment, over the course of several weeks, killed 898 Japanese soldirs, though they took but seven prisoners.[218] Filipino losses were high and as the Eighth Army report noted:

> The success of the USAFIP, NL, guerillas in driving the Japanese from the roads into the mountains was paid for by a higher casualty rate than would have been suffered by experience American troops under the same circumstances; for although they were aided by American artillery and planes, the Filipino forces lacked much of the special equipment required for the assault on prepared positions.[219]

Despite the above comments, the Filipino units performed an invaluable service in this generally unnecessary last weeks of the war. US units were tired. All involved in Eighth Army operations here had seen extended combat and lacked the strength to hold

---

216 Eighth Army, *Report of the Commanding General Eighth Army on the Luzon Mop-Up Operation* (Headquarters: Eighth Army, 1945), 17.

217 *Ibid.,* 22.

218 *Ibid.,* 26.

219 *Ibid.,* 28.

extended areas and continue to attack, even if those attacks were less costly and ferocious than previous ones. Not all parts of a successful army are combat troops and the Filipinos played their part.

The 32nd Infantry Division, which in May was pulled off the line because of losses and exhaustion, joined the Eighth Army in July and was directed to:

> secure the Baguio area and advance northward on Highway No. 11 until contact was established with the USAFIP, NL, guerillas near KM90. This maneuver was designed to open the highway as a supply route for the troops operating farter north and to bring pressure from the south on the enemy in the KM 90 – Bontoc – Bagabag area.[220]

Attacks, as with its brother divisions, were not unduly hindered by the Japanese. Artillery and armor did most of the work. Several months earlier the 32nd had labored on the Villa Verde Trail. The terrain here was equally forbidding, but the Japanese were no longer the same enemy. Advances continued until August 15, when hostilities officially ended.

In central Luzon, the 38th Infantry Division bore responsibility for Eighth Army operations. They patrolled, but most activity was to "support, control, and administer guerilla forces, and operate composite American and guerilla combat patrols in the western foothills of the southern Sierra Madre range."[221] Despite the limited US involvement they helped account for, in total, 20,311 Japanese dead and 2,396 prisoners. US losses in the Luzon mop-up operation were 36 dead and 607 wounded.[222] The ground war in the Pacific was over.

---

220 *Ibid.,* 30.

221 *Ibid.,* 31.

222 *Ibid.,* 35.

VIII

CONCLUSION

The Eighth Army, in terms of time, had the shortest existence of any US Army of WWII. Activated in the last days of 1944, it contributed to the war effort for approximately seven months, although its most concentrated effort occurred between April and June 1945. What was accomplished? In contributing to the ultimate US victory in the Pacific, very little. The Eighth began operations on Leyte, finishing off or, to use the phrase seen throughout this work, "mopping up" those Japanese left by the US Sixth Army, which made the initial landing and defeated the major enemy forces on the island. In essence, every operation undertaken by Eighth Army was a mop-up. Panay, Negros, or any of the other islands of the Southern Philippines evolved into fights with dug-in Japanese forces that did nothing to thwart the opening moments of the landings. What were the invasions of the Southern Philippines but large-scale mopping-up operations? Every island the Eighth Army landed on was rendered strategically useless the moment Sixth Army landed on Leyte in October 1944. The landings on Luzon in January 1945 pushed the Southern Philippines further into the periphery: they were not needed as air bases or staging areas. MacArthur had bypassed Japanese strongpoints during his strategically brilliant movement across New Guinea in 1944. The islands of the Southern Philippines could have been bypassed, their garrisons left to wither until war's end. For MacArthur, whose pride was sullied when forced out of the Philippines in 1942, to leave a square yard of the islands in Japanese hands was unfathomable. None of the islands Eichelberger and his Eighth Army attacked and secured mattered in the strategic military sense. Given the nature of the combat on these islands and the forbidding geography and horrendous weather, the cost was high:

	Killed	Wounded
Palawan	11	40
Zamboanga	220	665
Panay	20	50
Negros	381	1,061
Cebu	449	1,969
Mindanao	820	2,880[223]

All of the above losses were unnecessary. The operations themselves were unnecessary. The soldiers of the US divisions that fought here did so gallantly and skillfully. While their own losses were heavy, they inflicted far more casualties upon their enemy than they received. They deserve more recognition than history has bestowed upon them.

Why the "Forgotten Army?" They are essentially a footnote in the larger ground campaign to defeat the Japanese and entered the war in its final moments. When one thinks of the Pacific War, the great naval battles of Midway and Leyte Gulf burst to mind. The land battles on Guadalcanal, Iwo Jima, Okinawa, and even Manila would be the first out of one's mouth in any discussion. How often will Negros, Cebu City, or Davao even enter a discussion? For the men who fought in the Southern Philippines, many of them seasoned combat veterans, the fighting here was as hard as any they experienced in the war.

The Eighth Army did not fade away as did so many other US military formations at the end of the war. They occupied Japan and directed US efforts in the Korean War. They are better known for that than their efforts in WWII.

---

223 Losses at Leyte and Luzon are not included because they were part of an ongoing operation preceding the creation of the Eighth Army.

IX

Unpublished Sources

All of the unpublished sources in this study came from the Modern Military Records section of the National Archives in College Park, Maryland. Of the various units covered, some kept better wartime records than others. There is no greater resource for the firsthand accounts than these records offer.

Eighth Army. *Report Of The Commanding General Eighth US Army ON The Leyte-Samar Operation (Including Clearing of the Visayan Passage), 26 December1944–8 May 1945.* Headquarters: Eighth US Army, 1945.

———. *Report Of The Commanding General Eighth US Army On The Mindoro-Marinduque Operation, 1 January–31 January 1945.* Headquarters: Eighth US Army, 1945.

———. *Report Of The Commanding General Eighth US Army On The Palawan and Zamboanga Operation.* Headquarters: Eighth US Army, 1945.

———. *Report Of The Commanding General Eighth US Army On The Panay-Negros and Cebu Operations, Victor I and II.* Headquarters: Eighth US Army, 1945.

———. *Report Of The Commanding General Eighth US Army On The Mindanao Operation, Victor V.* Headquarters: Eighth US Army, 1945.

———. *Report Of The Commanding General Eighth US Army On The Luzon Mop-up Operation.* Headquarters: Eighth US Army, 1945.

General Headquarters Southwest Pacific Areas, Military Intelligence Section, General Staff. *Daily Intelligence Assessments and Summaries.*

Nineteenth Infantry Regiment. *Combat History Of The Nineteenth Infantry Regiment: Mindanao, P.I., 17 April 45-5 July 45.* Headquarters: Nineteenth Infantry Regiment, 1945.

Theater Judge Advocate. General Headquarters: United States Army Forces, Pacific, Office Of The Theater Judge Advocate, War Crimes Branch. *Atrocities at Puerto Princess, Palawan.* 18 August 1945.

——. *Murder of two American prisoners of war and five Filipino civilians on 26 March 1945 by members of Japanese Kempei Tai.* 16 October 1945.

——. *Murder of three Filipino civilians at Danao, Cebu, P.I.* 20 November 1945.

——. *Murder of Palicte Family on or about 26 March 1945, Cebu City.* 21 November 1945.

——. *Murder of Members of the Jaguren Family andOothers on 7 November 1944.* 28 November 1945.

——. *Murder and Raping of Civilians and Burning of Civilian Homes at Tubog, Minglanilla, Cebu, P.I., on 30 and 31 January 1945.* 29 November 1945.

——. *The Beating, Starvation and Torture of Tia Tian by Members of the Japanese Military Police from 3 April 1944 to 18 May 1944.* 30 November 1945.

——. *Murder, Torture, and Rape in the Towns of Ajuy and Sara, Iloilo Province, P.I., between 13 September 1943 and 29 September 1943.* 15 December 1945.

——. *Murder, Attempted Murder, Torture, and Attempted Rape of Civilians at Carcan, Cebu, P.I.* 18 December 1945.

——. *Murder of Filipino Civilians at Miagao, Iloilo Province, Panay, P.I.* 18 December 1945.

——. *Murder and rape of Filipino civilians in Davao City, Mindanao, P.I., in May 1945.* 8 January 1946.

——. *Murders at Ilang-Ilang and Bunawan, Davao, Mindanao, P.I., between 14 May 1945 and 15 June 1945.* 9 January 1946.

X Xorps. *History of X Corps on Mindanao, 17 April 45–30 June 45.* Headquarters: X Corps, 1945.

XXIV Corps. *Operations Report: XXIV Corps, Leyte, 26 December1944–10 February 1945.* Headquarters: XXIV Corps, 1945.

Sixth Infantry Division. *After Action Report: Final Phase Of Luzon Campaign, 1 July To 21 August 1945.* Headquarters: Sixth Infantry Division, 1945.

Seventh Infantry Division. *Operations Report: 7th Infantry Division, King II.* Headquarters: Seventh Infantry Division, 1945.

21st Infantry Regiment. *Mindanao: A Regiment In Action.* Headquarters: 21st Infantry Regiment, 24th Infantry Division. *Report After Combat: 21st Infantry Regiment, 17 April – 30 June 1945.* Headquarters: 21st Infantry Regiment, 24th Infantry Division, 1945.

24th Infantry Division. *Mindanao: Historical Report of the 24th Infantry Division.* Headquarters: 24th Infantry Division, 1945.

25th Infantry Division. *After Action Report, Medical Services Annex.* Headquarters: 25th Infantry Division, 1945.

32nd Infantry Division. *After Action Report, Annex#1, G-1 Report.* Headquarters: 32nd Infantry Division, 1945.

34th Infantry Regiment. *Historical Report Of The Mindanao Operation, 17 April–7 July 1945.* Headquarters: 34th Infantry Regiment, 24th Infantry Division, 1945.

40th Infantry Division. *Operations Report: 18 March-20 June 45.*

Victor I: Panay, Victor II: Negros. Headquarters, 40th Infantry Division, 1945.

124th Infantry Regiment. *Historical Record of the Mindanao Campaign.* Headquarters: 124th Infantry Regiment, 31st Infantry Division.

155th Infantry Regiment. *History: Mindanao, April-June 1945.* Headquarters: 155th Infantry Regiment, 31st Infantry Division.

163rd Infantry Regiment. *Historical Reports: V-4 Operation: Zamboanga.* Headquarters: 163rd Infantry Regiment, 41st Infantry Division, 1945.

305th Infantry Regiment. *A/A RPT – Leyte Campaign – 305th Infantry Regiment, 77th Infantry Division, 26 December 44–2 February 45.* Headquarters: 305th Infantry Regiment, 77th Infantry Division, 1945.

PUBLISHED SOURCES

All of the below sources are available through normal digital and traditional libraries. The immesaurable assistance provided by Robert Ross Smith's *Triumph In The Philippines* cannot be overstated. It is essentially a primary source. Mr. Smith interviewed many of those involved in the actual battles, including Japanese prisoners, and was able to give an outstanding overall appraisal of the entire Philippine campaign, not just the section that was covered here.

40th Infantry Division. *The Years of World War II.* Washington, DC: Army & Navy Publishing Company, 1947.

Cannon, M. Hamlin. *Leyte: The Return To The Philippines.* Washington, DC: Center of Military History, 1954.

Cronin, Francis. *Under the Southern Cross: The Saga of the Americal Division.* Washington, DC: Combat Forces Presss, 1981.

Eichelberger, Robert L. *Our Jungle Road To Tokyo.* New York: The Viking Press, 1950.

Etzler, Charles R., Lt. Colonel. *The Japanese Defense Of The Island of Negros (Occidental) P.I.* Fort Leavenworth, Kansas: Command and General Staff College, 1947.

Flanagan, Edward M., Jr. *The Angels: A History Of The 11th Airborne Division, 1943-1946.* Washington, DC: Infantry Journal Press, 1948.

Frank, Richard. *Guadalcanal.* New York: Penguin Books, 1990.

Leary, William M. (Editor). *We Shall Return: MacArthur's Coomanders And The Defeat of Japan.* Lexington: The University Press of Kentucky, 1988.

Luvaas, Jay. *Dear Miss Em: General Eichelberger's War in the Pacific: 1942–1945.* New York: Praeger Publishers, 1972.

MacArthur, Douglas. *Reminiscences.* Annapolis: Naval Institute Press, 1964.

McCartney, William F. *The Jungleers: A History Of The 41st Infantry Division.* Washington, DC: The 41st Infantry Division Association, 1948.

Muehrcke, Robert C. *Orchids In The Mud: Personal Accounts By Veterans Of The 132nd Infantry Regiment.* Chicago: J.S. Printing, 1985.

Schaller, Michael. *Douglas MacArthur: The Far Eastern General.* London: Oxford University Press, 1989.

Smith, Robert Ross. *Triumph In The Philippines.* Washington, DC: Center of Military History, 1963.

Enough cannot be said of the value of this work. Robert Ross Smith interviewed all relevant personnel on both sides of the battle after the war, provides the best maps and overlays of the plans and battles, and offers insightful, fact-based assessments. Nothing remotely tied to this subject can ever be undertaken without first reading this book.

Van der Vat, Dan. *The Pacific Campaign*. New York: Simon & Schuster, 1991.

Young, Robert. *They Too Fought The Japanese*. New York: City University of New York, 2003.

Pacific Hurtgen: The American Army In Northern Luzon, 1945. Washington, DC: Westphalia Press, 2017.

Maps/Illustrations

p. 59: Robert Ross Smith, *Triumph In The Philippines*, 594, Courtesy of the Department of Defense

p. 68: Robert Ross Smith, *Triumph In The Philippines*, 603, Courtesy of the Department of Defense

p. 77: Robert Ross Smith, *Triumph In The Philippines*, 611, Courtesy of the Department of Defense

p. 91: Robert Ross Smith, *Triumph In The Philippines*, 640, Courtesy of the Department of Defense

p. 92: Robert Ross Smith, *Triumph In The Philippines*, 639, Courtesy of the Department of Defense

p. 94: Robert Ross Smith, *Triumph In The Philippines*, 624, Courtesy of the Department of Defense

p. 102: Robert Ross Smith, *Triumph In The Philippines*, 631, Courtesy of the Department of Defense

p. 120: Robert Ross Smith, *Triumph In The Philippines*, 565, Courtesy of the Department of Defense

Made in the USA
Coppell, TX
01 September 2020

35966478R00085